To Tamsin,
All my best!

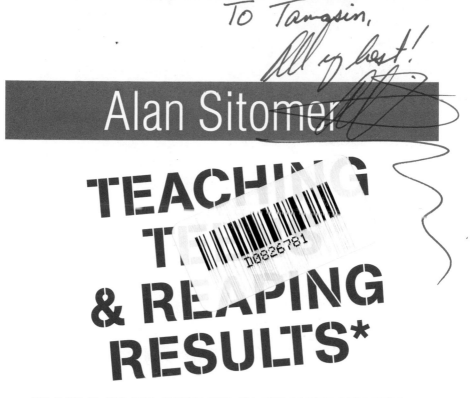

Alan Sitomer

TEACHING
TEENS
& REAPING
RESULTS*

*IN A WI-FI, HIP-HOP, WHERE-HAS-ALL-THE-SANITY-GONE WORLD

Stories, Strategies, Tools & Tips From a Three-Time Teacher of the Year Award Winner

foreword by Jim Burke

📖 SCHOLASTIC

New York • Toronto • London • Auckland • Sydney
Mexico City • New Delhi • Hong Kong • Buenos Aires

for Sienna

Editor: Lois Bridges
Production: Melissa L. Inglis-Elliott
Cover photograph: Rene Macura
Cover design by Brian LaRossa
Interior photographs: Alan Sitomer and Rene Macura
Interior design by Holly Grundon

ISBN-13: 978-0-545-03603-0
ISBN-10: 0-545-03603-8

Printed in the U.S.A.
1 2 3 4 5 6 7 8 9 10   23   14 13 12 11 10 09

This is a book for teachers who want to go somewhere meaningful and special.

 —Dr. Bill Younglove
  Recipient of the National Council of Teachers of English
  High School Excellence Award

A book that should be added to the library of every educator, both novice and veterans alike!

 —Kimberly Kyff
  2007 Michigan Teacher of the Year, Detroit Public Schools, NBCT

I teach in a grade 7–12 school where 100 percent of the children are eligible for free lunch. Thank you for writing a book that helps teachers meet each student at the place where each student is instead of playing the blame game.

 —Kim Schaefer
  2007 Utah Teacher of the Year, NBCT

This book should be required reading for new and veteran teachers alike.

 —Lois Rebich
  2007 Pennsylvania Teacher of the Year

This book is a must-read for any educator who wants to move beyond the traditional approach that continues to under serve our students. It's a text that will revolutionize your thinking and give you the instructional tools needed to encourage, engage, and empower your students.

 —Lee-Ann Stephens
  2006 Minnesota Teacher of the Year

Guaranteed to enable all teachers to do what teachers do best… teach from the heart not from a mere text. Sitomer's insights will bring both laughter and tears to every reader.

 —Marlene Srock
  2007 North Dakota State Teacher of the Year

My husband and I combined have 70 years of teaching experience and we found this book to not only be on target, but to split the bull's-eye. This book says it all!

 —Jan Keese
  2007 Iowa Teacher of the Year

Finally, a tell-it-like-it-should-be-pedagogy filled with hope and vision that cuts right on through the edu-babble and makes educators want to pick up the chalk!

 —J. Bradley Minnick, Ph.D.
  Director of English Education, University of Arkansas at Little Rock

Contents

Foreword

Every time we get the chance, Alan and I go out for dinner—always sushi—and spend the whole night talking about the kids we teach, books, and education, three passions we share. Last time we got together we went out for dessert and ordered what was the biggest piece of cake either of us had ever seen. That "slice" reminds me of the book you hold in your hands: dense, delicious, and even a bit dangerous.

Alan is the real deal. He goes into class every day to address and wrestle with the challenges we all face. Though some of the realities are daunting, in the midst of these is a man who brings with him a generous laugh, a quick smile, a big heart, high expectations, and a quick mind, all of which he uses to help his students at Lynwood High achieve what many believe they cannot.

"Mr. Alan," as his students call him, is a bit dangerous in that he doesn't accept the way things are but works to turn what *is* into what *could be*. He does this by holding his students to high standards that they and others might at first think they cannot reach. Like that big piece of cake we ordered, which no one around us thought we could eat, Alan shows them that one bite at a time, one can accomplish anything. Instead of saying his students cannot read and understand Dylan Thomas and advanced literary devices, he brings in Tupac Shakur's rap music to show them what they already know, then teaches them how to use that to figure out and talk about what they don't (yet) understand.

Such demanding instruction yields results we can all envy and applaud: more than 95 percent of his students passed the English Language Arts section of the California High School Exit Exam on their first attempt at the test; 100 percent of his AVID (Advancement via Individual Determination) seniors graduated from a Title I school where the Title I statewide average for entering freshman leaving school by senior year with a diploma hovers between 55 and 60 percent. Alan's kids enter the world armed with brains and faith in themselves.

One of Alan's favorite books is Stephen Covey's *The 7 Habits of Highly Effective People* (2004). As Covey does through his books, Alan teaches kids how to succeed not only in school but in the world for which we prepare them. Unlike Covey, however, Alan offers 107 habits of effective people; as you will quickly learn, my friend Alan is a man of great passion and wonderful excess who wants to share not just that big piece of cake but the recipe for it so you can bake your own.

Teaching Teens and Reaping Results in a Wi-Fi, Hip-Hop, Where-Has-All-the-Sanity-Gone World is not a book of recipes, but rather a book of principles, ideals, and lessons that Alan has developed from his years in the classroom at Lynwood High. We get not only useful strategies and techniques but the story of where those ideas come from and how they play out in the classroom and the lives of his kids. In addition to these stories and strategies, Alan offers—I can't resist extending the metaphor—like a delicious cherry on top of the cake, helpful suggestions and resources in the appendices, everything from recommended books that kids will definitely read to suggestions for getting them to do their homework.

In my book *The Teacher's Essential Guide: Effective Instruction* (2008), I identified the principles of effective teachers across subject areas. While Alan gets up to teach English every day, his work here is relevant to all teachers of all subjects. Every page reflects the principles I found in my research on effective teachers. On every page you will also find Alan working to overcome the challenges we all face every day we walk into that classroom. As you read about his struggles and successes, you will not only learn how he does it but be inspired by the knowledge that it *can* be done, and that success—great, real success—is possible if we ask as much of ourselves and our students as Alan does.

—Jim Burke

Acknowledgments and Shout-Outs

Let me be clear: Without the tireless, intelligent, constant, and outstanding efforts of **Lois Bridges**, this book would not be the text that it is. Above all, she is the reason this manuscript exists in the fashion that it does and if you find any excellence at all inside these pages, know that it most assuredly is owed to the heart, mind, and wonderfully great character of Lois Bridges. I am forever indebted to you, Lois, for your insight, passion, and consummate professionalism. (Plus, you're really nice.) *Thank you so much!* (Especially for saving me from myself.)

Obviously, I need to give a big ol' shout-out to a host of other incredible people who lent their support, talent, brains, and heart to the publication of this work. In no particular order, I'd like to thank:

- Melissa Inglis-Elliott, production editor extraordinaire, who brought her A-game to the playing field for this one . . . *no doubt!*

- Gloria Pipkin, hawk-eyed senior editor, who challenged, probed, and simply made this a better, more disciplined, more competent, and weighty book.

- Brian LaRossa, cover designer. Have you seen the cover? *Off the hook!* Thanks tons, Dude.

- Jaime Lucero, art director. *Uh, hello, have you seen this book?* Wow! Thank you so much as well!

- Nelson Hitchcock, director of strategic marketing, the man with a forever crooked ear from me bending it on and on and on.

- Dick Robinson, president of Scholastic, the Big Boss who is salt of the earth and makes all teachers feel appreciated for the noble work being done in our nation's classrooms.

- Terry Cooper, former vice-president of teaching resources (now retired), who helped me join the Scholastic team.

- Virginia Dooley, editorial director of teaching resources and a class act through and through, who is unwavering in her dedication to excellence.

- Eileen Hillebrand, vice-president of marketing for teaching resources, the lady with the gusto to go big; a wizard of wit, knowledge, and insight.

- Susan Kolwicz, senior marketing manager of teaching resources, and a person whom I felt like I knew for a hundred years on the very first day we met.

- Ray Coutu, managing editor, perpetual supporter, and 100 percent stand-up guy.

- Beth Tripp, copyeditor, who *maKes* mE loook ReAlly *gooood*, really often.

- Renée Nicholls, a proofreader who proves that the proofreading really is in the pudding (whatever that means).

- Amy Rowe, editorial coordinator, who helped make so many behind-the-scenes wheels turn.

- Readers: Jennifer Abrams, Noah Borrero, Shawn Bird, Jane Buch-binder, Sandra Wilde, Sarah Galvin—a crew of people who offered insights along the way that greatly helped me shape, form, and elevate the manuscript in a host of significant ways.

Of course, without Al Zuckerman, the agent, there is no Alan Sitomer, the writer. A big shout-out to Al and all the gang at Writers House.

And last, but most certainly not least, I want to give a *huge thanks* to Jim Burke for, well, everything. If only all teachers in America were lucky enough to have a peer such as Jim in their lives, our schools and students would be a thousand times better off for it. He not only makes me a better educator but a better, more reflective, and purposeful human being, and I am proud to call him my friend. *Much love to ya, JB!*

Introduction

I teach in a community plagued by gangs, guns, and drugs. I've also taught in a community plagued by BMWs, Gold Cards, and, yep, you guessed it, drugs. If there is one thing I have learned between having students who come from Compton and others who come from Beverly Hills, it's that teens are teens are teens. Anyone who tells you differently is full of pelican poop.

Now, usually I'm not so dogmatic about my opinions, but when it comes to today's kids, the stakes are simply too high not to be blunt. Matter of fact, I feel the stakes are so high that working toward the betterment of today's teenagers has become the preeminent focus of my career. Happily, through my work as both an author and an educator, I've had a small degree of positive influence. Sadly, I know it's not enough.

So I wrote this book.

Inside, you'll meet my students, discover my strategies, and hear our stories. However, be forewarned. While my own personal journey reads somewhat like a Hollywood movie, this is not a "Kumbaya"-style book where everything works out all rosy for the kids. The simple truth is that scathing dangers lurk for today's teens. And not all of them escape unscathed.

Some never even had a chance.

In my estimation, the current generation of teenagers, whether you love them, hate them, or simply think they are an unintelligible scourge rained down upon us by a vindictive alien deity, are being forced to make some very adult choices about some very adult matters with some very adult consequences hanging in the balance. And quite often these kids are being asked to make these choices by the ripe old age of 15 . . . if not sooner.

It's terrifying.

It's also terrifically exciting. Why? Because as a keen philosopher once pointed out, with danger comes opportunity, and I am of the firm belief that today's teens have the opportunity not only to navigate the dangerous maze of contemporary adolescence but also to prosper immensely from the challenges of their journey.

And if they prosper, we will all prosper. However, before they can succeed, today's teenagers need to be empowered with tools that enable them to thrive: tools for success in the classroom as well as in life.

This book is the recounting of my search for, and discovery of, those tools. I wrote it with the hope that you would not only be entertained, enlightened, and inspired but also be inclined—no, not be inclined, feel *compelled*—to pass along the worthwhile insights you glean from these pages. Today's teens desperately need it.

Today's teens desperately need you.

Look in your heart. You know I'm right.

I hope you enjoy the book.

Alan Lawrence Sitomer
Written in the Lynwood High School Library

Häagen-Daz, Hip-Hop, and Holy Smokes!
Teaching Teens to Bounce Back

I will never forget the Sunday night before my first day as an inner-city high school English teacher. Fantastical visions of academic splendor, peer camaraderie, and intellectually hungry students on fire with scholarly drive as I awakened my classes to the power and magic of literature raced through my head (all to the soundtrack of the movie *Lean on Me*, of course).

Then, on Monday morning, reality hit. Actually, it didn't just hit, it smacked me in the face, kicked me in the groin, and made me want to call in sick for the next 179 days. My students, I discovered, would rather visit the dentist than immerse themselves in the classic curriculum of English class. What was I to do?

I did what many who are faced with perplexing dilemmas do. I denied there was a problem, buried my head underneath the gum-stained carpet, and spent many, many classroom hours trying to force a very square peg into a very round hole. After all, I had to teach the classics, didn't I? I mean, they had been taught to me. And the people who taught them to me had had them taught to them. I wasn't just an educator; I was a torch bearer, an illuminator of wisdom, the last defense against illiteracy, anarchy, and the apocalypse.

To deviate would be heresy!

Okay, okay, I have a bit of a flair for the dramatic, but still, what the *bleep* was I supposed to do? All I knew was what they taught me at How-to-Be-a-Teacher school, and let me tell you, on the practical scale of dealing with real kids in real classrooms, this was proving to be the proverbial screen door on a submarine.

After much arguing with myself about the course I should take, I decided to choose the path of the mythological hero: I'd become the English-teacher version of Sisyphus, pushing a book up a hill I knew was going to roll right the heck back down. "So what?" I thought. "At least I'll be teaching the classics." It wasn't long before frustration, disillusionment, and aggravation took over. My kids hated the books I was asking them to read.

Sure, I could have flunked my students for not doing their assigned work, but I soon learned that for many kids in the inner city, if I threatened them with an F in English class, they'd simply laugh at me, taking the attitude "An F in English? Yo, dude, get in line. I'm already failing history, math, science. . . ."

Finally, I decided to follow in the footsteps of another great pedagogical tradition, doing what many educators do at some point in their fine and distinguished careers. I went home, took out a spoon, and gobbled down a few containers of Häagen-Dazs ice cream. (I swear there's magic in those fattening little buckets.) Then, hung over from a sugar overload, I returned to school the next day determined to delve deeply into the question of why my students were so reluctant to read.

Actually, the word *reluctant* is a euphemism. My students overtly hated books. And why not, I soon discovered. Many of them read years below their grade level, suffered a personal history of unequivocal failure with the written word, and had been perpetually ostracized, shamed, and belittled for their lack of ability to work with typed, black ink on a flat, rectangular page ever since they could remember.

Action-adventure movies? Now those spoke to them. Downloading music while chatting mindlessly on their cell phones? Now that engaged them. Deconstructing fiction as we analyzed the literary device of alliteration? Some days I could actually hear the snoring before their heads hit the desks.

Then one day, I came up with the idea of using hip-hop. It was a decision that would change my life.

I turned to hip-hop because I understood the profound need to do something significant to reshape my students' perspective on reading. Not something small to merely alter their viewpoint; I'm talking about needing to do something radical to shift their entire mind-set toward books.

And why shoot for such an immense alteration of their mind-set?

Because as a classroom teacher, I knew a dirty little secret.

The fact is that the foremost indicator of teens who are at risk in our society boils down to a tremendously simple statistic. It's not socioeconomic status. It's not race or gender. It's not whether a child grows up with two married parents living in the same home. It's none of these. The number one determinant of whether or not kids will eventually navigate their way safely through the dangerous maze of adolescence can be boiled down to a very simple question: Do they read?

> Kids who read with proficiency are empowered with essential skills they'll need to survive the demands of contemporary life. And kids who don't read are at risk. It's that simple.

Just ask yourself, "Do they read?"

Kids who read with proficiency are empowered with essential skills they'll need to survive the demands of contemporary life. And kids who don't read are at risk. It's that simple.

Nonreading teens, as dozens of studies have proven, are significantly more likely to be involved in violence, crime, weapons, unwanted pregnancies, and drugs. The U.S. Department of Health knows it. The U.S. Department of Education knows it. The Federal Bureau of Prisons most certainly knows it. It seems as though the only people who don't know it are the folks in the media who keep perpetuating the idea that at-risk teen behavior has something to do with the color of a kid's skin or the amount of money his parents earn (or do not earn) for a living.

Nonsense!

Literacy skills are like canaries in the coal mines—as soon as they start to go belly up, there is big trouble ahead.

Essentially, as an inner-city classroom educator, I found myself with a unique vantage point. On one hand, I understood the staggering significance of the need for teens to read, while at the same time, I was witnessing an immense disinterest in and disengagement from literature by teens in my very own English class. It didn't take a genius to see that reading was under full-fledged assault from a variety of well-financed enemy armies.

There were violent video games. There were reality television shows. There were the Internet, the iPod, the cellular telephone, movies, text messaging, and a host of other societal forces so fiercely competing for my kids' attention that I soon found myself sounding like a crotchety old grandfather grousing, "You know, when I was a kid. . . . "

Something, I knew, had to be done.

Hold on, let me rephrase that. It wasn't that something *had* to be done, it was that *I* had to do something—and there's a world of difference between those two statements.

I decided to focus my energies on searching for and providing solutions. And the solution, as I saw it, could be the creation of an accessible, relevant, engaging curriculum that validated the students' personal interests while simultaneously teaching the state-mandated classroom objectives.

Yep, I decided to bust out some hip-hop.

Of course, in hindsight, turning to contemporary music in order to spark my students' interest in reading and the language arts makes complete sense, but at the time when I first began, it came off as a radical and an unwelcome idea to the powers that be, so I found myself working with hip-hop almost surreptitiously. There were a few reasons for that.

First, as a youngish teacher, fairly new to Lynwood High School, I was concerned about what my peers on the staff, in administration, and in the broader field of education would think. Using hip-hop in the classroom—come on, that wasn't considered *real* teaching. That was just screwin' around, right? Second, bringing hip-hop into the class could be construed as validating a violent, misogynistic, bling-bling lifestyle. Foes, I knew, no matter how good my intentions nor how strong my arguments, would be plentiful. This was the moment that I decided that everything I would do with hip-hop in the classroom would be entirely free of profanity, homophobia, and misogyny. In truth, I saw these terms as great vocabulary words I could teach to my kids with a ton of wonderful ideas to explore, but come on, I told myself, this ain't MTV I'm doing here. That's why I immediately set a high standard for what was appropriate for classroom use and made sure not to deviate from this academic line.

And so, being a firm believer that it's better to beg forgiveness than ask permission, I started searching far and wide for a way to create an original language arts lesson plan for my class based on the musical lyrics my students were so crazy about, in spite of my reservations about how I would be perceived by the world outside my classroom. The stakes, as I saw them, were just too high not to try something to help my kids.

That's when Tupac Shakur, Dylan Thomas, and LaToya Johnson showed me the true power of teaching teens and reaping results in a wi-fi, hip-hop, where-has-all-the-sanity-gone world.

Tupac Shakur you've probably heard of. He was a hip-hop megastar. Dylan Thomas is a renowned poet whose works we often find in the ridiculously thick language arts textbooks we are provided with for our English classes. LaToya Johnson I am quite confident you don't know. She was one of 38 students I had in my third-period English class. (That's right, public school classes like mine all across the country are horrifically huge. And they're quite often populated with kids who are years below grade level in terms of their academic skills and years ahead of grade level in terms of their knowledge of sexuality and community violence. More on that later.)

Essentially, the further I explored the idea of using hip-hop as a bridge to a classic poem, my academic objective of the day, the more I realized the great many possibilities that lay in front of me. Tupac, I discovered as I read over a "clean" section of his lyrics taken from a piece called "Me Against the World" (once again, to be clear: no profanity, no misogyny, and no homophobia), used literary devices such as metaphors to craft his work. Hey, so did Dylan Thomas. Tupac's work also had a theme. Whoa, so did Dylan Thomas's. Additionally, Tupac's work had rhyme scheme, subtext, and tone, much like the work of Dylan Thomas. "Oh my goodness," I thought, "we'll do a lesson identifying poetic literary devices."

Soon the wheels in my head started turning and I elevated my academic ambitions. "Hey, we can employ the time-honored English class tradition of comparing and contrasting ideas," I told myself. Minutes later I recognized that I was ascending Bloom's famous taxonomy of learning. Before long, I had devised a way for my students to analyze, interpret, hypothesize, and speculate about a host of ideas raised in connection with the two pieces of "poetry" I was planning to study.

"Oh my goodness," I suddenly realized. "We can even cover the standards!"

I couldn't help but laugh. The standards are our classroom academic curriculum objectives as set forth by the state, and here I was discovering a means by which I could use the most vilified art form on the planet—hip-hop—as a tool to educate the supposedly most unreachable youth of our nation—urban teens.

Holy smokes, I was on fire!

It took me until two o'clock in the morning to finish my lesson plan, but I just knew in my bones that this crazy hip-hop idea was going to work.

And it did.

I walked into my room and as soon as the bell rang, I asked, "Who wants to study some hip-hop?" Immediately, I had 100 percent engagement from 100 percent of the students. Even the kids in the back row, you know the kind—the asocial, mute, antidisestablishmentarianists who always wear sweatshirt hoodies draped over their heads like Obi-Wan Kenobi from *Star Wars*. It turned out that these young people were not stricken with a rare tongue disease that prevented vocalization at all. In fact, it turned out they were intelligent, thoughtful, passionate students with definite points of view on a whole host of topics.

And suddenly they'd become eager to share. My teens had become engaged. Authentically.

Once I got da' hip-hop rollin' (hey, you gotta use da' slang), class was magic. I was like one of those dice shooters in Vegas who was just hot, hot, hot. Nothing I could do was wrong. Ideas, debates, full participation from every kid in the class—I had it all. And though I had prepared a range of class activities that day that extended beyond an analysis of the poetic literary devices commonly used by each of the texts being compared and contrasted, one simple handout I passed along (see next page) lit the room on fire.

Kids chimed in about race. Kids railed out against institutionalized oppression. Kids brought up Hurricane Katrina, Elvis Presley, Luciano Pavarotti, O. J. Simpson, and jazz musicians of the Harlem Renaissance. And even though getting kids to read and respond to every other handout I'd ever produced prior to this class had felt like extracting stringy pumpkin guts with my bare hands during Halloween carving time, during this class I was on the exact opposite end of the spectrum, feeling more like some sort of justice o' the peace who had lost control of his courtroom, shouting, "Order in the court!" as I tried my darnedest to rein in all the

Think carefully about the issue presented in the following paragraph before responding.

Dylan Thomas is a celebrated poet who has received widespread acknowledgment and multiple accolades for his literary efforts. Tupac Shakur, outside of the musical world of pop music and hip-hop, has received few if any accolades and little recognition for his literary skill and ability by the same people who recognize Dylan Thomas as one of America's premier wordsmiths.

Question: Do you feel the work of contemporary hip-hop poets (in general) gets the positive recognition it deserves? Does the work of contemporary artists ever get the recognition it deserves, or do years have to pass before the merits of their efforts are recognized?

enthusiasm and create a space whereby people could be heard instead of shouting over one another. And then, when the bell finally rang to end the period, some of my students were even still so involved in heated discussions that they carried their classroom conversations right out into the hall. As any teacher knows, when what you're doing inside of class makes its way to the outside of class, you've just hit the daily double.

My hip-hop lesson plan had worked.

I went home that night on a teacher's high, exhausted yet thrilled all at the same time. See, that's the thing about educators. Though we want money like the rest of humanity, we don't do our jobs solely for the paycheck. We'll put up with the abuse from the politicians. We'll put up with the meltdowns of the parents. We'll put up with the senseless mandates of the administration, the preposterous lack of resources, the unimaginable overcrowding, and the general dysfunction of the American educational system. We'll put up with it all—all of it—as long as we are not cut off from that inimitable sensation of the teacher's high that we get from connecting with kids. The truth is every bit of the aggravation and frustration we educators endure is made entirely worthwhile by this feeling.

Matter of fact, it's why we keep coming back. We love to teach! And when we do and that lightbulb goes off for our students, there is nothing better.

Nothing.

(Basically, I pity accountants. Then again, accountants, when they see my salary, pity me, so it's an even swap.)

Anyway, my hip-hop idea had worked, my wife was very proud, and I zonked out that night like a bear. Then the next day, I walked into class, and guess what my students wanted to do?

That's right, more.

"More?" I said. "Do you have any idea what it took me just to prepare for yesterday? I mean, this isn't the *VH1 Rap Video Awards Show* I'm doing up here."

It was, however, at this moment that I realized I was standing at a precipice, a place between two worlds. It was, and I don't use this word lightly, my epiphany. Hip-hop could be used as a tool to revolutionize academic success for disengaged teens while building a bridge to the classic curriculum of the language arts class. What's more, through hip-hop, I could tackle the mandated learning objectives of our state and nation.

"Whoa!" I thought. The rush of awareness was incredible. But it wasn't until the very last day of school that year when LaToya Johnson walked into my room that I fully grasped the significance of using hip-hop in my class.

Now, at Lynwood High, the very last day of the school year is not an academic day. Half, if not less, of the students show up, and those who do only do so to say good-bye, spend a final day with their friends, and maybe pick up their grades. But LaToya had come for a different purpose. She came to give me a note.

Actually, LaToya didn't hand me the note; she just kind of slid a folded piece of paper across my desk, then quietly said something like, "Have a nice summer, Mr. Alan," and walked out.

(By the way, I go by Mr. Alan, not Mr. Sitomer, with my students. It's less formal and helps build a better bond. And when you work where I do, a person needs every little advantage he can get.)

As LaToya left, I thought to myself, "That was weird." I mean, LaToya obviously wanted me to read the note, but she also obviously did not want me to read the note in front of her. I put LaToya's folded-up piece of paper aside until I had a free moment later that day. Then, when I finally had a chance to read what she had written, my knees buckled.

As it turns out, two weeks prior to my hip-hop lesson, LaToya had been seriously thinking about committing suicide. (That's another thing I've learned as a teacher who works with teens: entertaining thoughts of seriously hurting themselves is almost a rite of passage for kids these days, especially for our girls. It's out of control!) However, that day we did the lesson on hip hop, LaToya "got" Dylan Thomas.

The poem we had read was one of his most famous works, a piece called "Do Not Go Gentle Into That Good Night." In this poem, Thomas has a line that he repeats over and over: "Rage, rage against the dying of the light."

In her note, LaToya explained that for the first time in her life, she "understood" a classic poem. Prior to my class she had always hated poetry and instantly tuned out whenever her English teachers inevitably turned to this section of the textbook. However, LaToya decided to give this Dylan Thomas poem a chance because Tupac Shakur was her favorite hip-hop artist, and when I informed the class that we were going to read some of Tupac's work as part of an academic activity, LaToya dropped her guard and gave it her all.

And full throttle for LaToya resulted in her discovering the deep meaning embedded in Thomas's poem (i.e., you've got to *rage, rage against the dying of the light*). That was my theme of the day, to explore how artists across the centuries have explicated in their own unique ways, "Yo, life is hard and you've got to suck it up and get back up on that horse once you've been thrown. Giving up in this world, no matter what has happened to you, is not an option!"

I told my students how there was not a single adult I knew who had not been kicked in the pit of the stomach by life at some point, yet somehow, somewhere, they had all learned to dig deep, to reach down, to get back up, and to forge on in spite of life's spectacular ability to dish out complicated and emotional pain.

That's what Tupac was talking about. That's what Dylan Thomas was talking about. That's why we study classic literature in the first place, I believe, because it's the place where the greatest thinkers in the history of humanity are passing down their wisdom, strength, and knowledge so we can find inspiration in our darkest nights and one day pass along the

lessons we learn to the next generation. The words and ideas of my class are not about stupid little bubble tests. English class, to me, is about the lifeblood of humanity!

That day LaToya got it. She really got it. So much so that she decided to "Rage, rage against the dying of the light" and not end her own life. LaToya, as she explained in her note, decided to live.

I sat back and realized that one of the biggest problems I face as an educator is that when you teach in classes as large as the ones I do, there is simply no way to know all of the things that are going on in all of your students' lives. Schools have, to some degree, become like a factory, with too many kids slipping through too many cracks despite the best efforts of many, many hardworking people. But hip-hop had allowed me to get through, to seal the cracks—in a way more powerful than anything I had ever possibly imagined. LaToya hadn't just read a poem; she had seen her own life reflected in the work of a celebrated literary artist and taken deep meaning from the text, so much so that it altered the course of her own future for the better.

Now that's the power of literature!

Right then I decided that if one little poem could do that much for a student, what if I could figure out a way to get my students to really read books? The effect could be incredible.

But where would I start?

Teach Teens to Bounce Back

Look, life is going to punch you in the mouth. It doesn't matter who you are, how much money you have, what color your skin is, or whether you have more athletic skill than any other human being who ever walked the planet. At some point, in some way, in some manner, life is gonna roll up and blast you with a straight right cross to the chin.

And it is going to hurt.

The real question each of us must face is "How am I going to respond?"

That's why the very first thing I teach teens is about the need to *bounce back!*

Society and our schools, in my opinion, completely misrepresent the way the real world works. The messages these institutions frequently send to teenagers are to avoid problems. To steer clear of trouble. To keep a safe distance out of harm's way.

Ha! Nobody escapes harm's way. Not Abe Lincoln. Not Albert Einstein. Not even Mother Teresa. This is why I strongly believe that stripping

"

Bounce back,
bay-bee! That's
the skill to teach
to teens.

teenagers of the delusion that somehow they are going to be spared from facing tough times is one of the best gifts a parent or teacher can offer to kids. Be straightforward. Tell your teens what I tell them: "Life will knock you down. The real question is ('cause hey, it's gut-check time) are you going to get back up?"

Being resolved to respond to life's challenges instead of seeking to avoid life's difficulties makes, in my professional opinion, all the difference in the world to a kid.

Don't think so? Just ask LaToya—her shift in perspective is what changed everything for her. If you noticed, LaToya's solution did not come from a remediation of the external forces that were driving her to take such an extreme course of action. Heck, I didn't even tell you what her problems were.

That's because I didn't need to. It was never the outside circumstances that left LaToya feeling suicidal; it was her inner fortitude that needed strengthening. Once Dylan Thomas spoke to and reinvigorated LaToya's inner strength—an inner strength that, by the way, was always there— LaToya rose from her despair more determined than ever to fight on for herself.

Kinda awesome, isn't it? And hey, guess what? All kids are built this way.

Bounce back, bay-bee! That's the skill to teach to teens.

As I often tell my students, successful people respond productively, proactively, and in a positive manner to adversity. Hardships don't beat them. Their mind-set is that they will beat hardship. That doesn't mean stuff doesn't hurt. It just means that successful people don't crumble, their lives don't fall apart, and they don't get spun permanently off track as a result of being knocked on their butt by, as Shakespeare would say, "the slings and arrows of outrageous fortune."

Basically, there seems to be a pattern to our world. At some point life is going to thump a person and then wait for the response. The thing most teens do not know is that people's internal responses to this thumping are almost always going to mean more than the external pounding they take. It's the response to the stimulus, not the stimulus itself, that matters most in our lives.

And that's really good news. Why? Because we all get to choose our response to life's difficulties. Some teens choose to whine and complain.

Some teens choose to squawk and moan. Some teens choose to complain about outside forces or blame others for their negative circumstances.

And some teens choose to fight. They choose to stand up, dig in, and bounce back. This is what I strive to teach the kids with whom I work and it's what I firmly believe more parents and teachers out there need to be teaching their teens, too.

Make it part of your educational curriculum.

Bouncin' back, it's the skill that kills.

Now, being that I'm pretty forthright with my kids, I'll put it right to them when times are tough for them. "Are you going to go out and slay these dragons? Are you going to go out and battle these forces of adversity? Do you have what it takes right here, right now, right at this moment to suck it up, reach down deep, and go out and grab yourself the brass ring?"

Inevitably teens, all teens, even abused, gangbanging, incarcerated teens (and I know, I've worked with them) invariably, when I ask this question, look into their hearts and on the inside, hear an inner voice scream, *"Oh, heck yes!"*

They may be nervous. They may be scared. They may have butterflies the size of seagulls floating in their stomachs, but inside they will be tingling because their inner strength will have been awakened, tapped, and challenged.

It is my firm belief that this inner strength is mankind's most irrepressible force, and as adults we must never forget that in the chest of every teen beats the heart of a hero. Look, if you are going to work with kids, this is a truth that you must never forget.

Never ever.

Matter of fact, it's your job to mine it. To speak to it. To foster it and nurture it.

Adversity shouldn't be a shock to teens, and resiliency, the determination to bounce back, should be a habit. In my opinion, this is the very first tool for teen success. Before there are goals, before there are challenges, before there are triumphs and achievements and glory, there is the knowledge of inevitable adversity and the comprehension that the greatest ally teens can have in this world is an unrelenting determination to bounce back from whatever curveballs life throws at them.

Because curveballs are gonna come . . . they come for all of us.

The cliché says, "When life gives you lemons, make lemonade." As I see it, too many kids are being admonished to avoid the lemons. Me, I say seek to turn your teens into a crew of lemonade makers who drink deeply from the well of adversity and find nourishment from the challenges of life.

Remember, successful teens bounce back. Teach this to your students and you will have taught them well.

Tips for Teaching Teens to Bounce Back

Shift the Language

As both an English teacher and an author, I know the power of words.

Change the word *problem* to the word *challenge*. Problems wear on us; they beat us down. Challenges ask for the best in us. They provide us an opportunity to shine, to do our best.

Help Kids Abandon a Woe-Is-Me Attitude

When teens find themselves facing challenging circumstances, a great many feel it must be their own fault, as if they did something wrong to be in such a tough spot. That leads to getting down on themselves, a mind-set that can be highly detrimental because it robs teens of their internal strength to respond to the challenges that lie in front of them.

Yes, it's important to reflect upon the *why* element of adversity. However, it's far too easy for teens to become paralyzed by the question of why as opposed to becoming responsible for addressing the more important issue of what to do next and how to best respond to the situation.

Tell your students to leave self-pity at the door. Teach teens to focus on working toward solutions instead of bemoaning the problems.

Watch for the Three Enemies of Bouncing Back

Not Getting Started

Challenges don't just go away, and the longer they lie unattended, the more formidable they become. Difficulties in this world are much more likely to snowball and grow as opposed to simply—and miraculously—just disappearing on their own. Start now.

Continuing to Make the Same Mistakes That Triggered the Difficulties in the First Place

Stimulus causes response. Action causes reaction. Participating in the same behaviors that created the original challenges is only going to create future challenges of the same, or of a more extreme, nature. As the old saying goes, "The only way to get out of a hole is to first stop digging."

Giving in to Despondency and Hopelessness

The ultimate enemy for teens is the enemy within: a lack of belief and hope. Without the faith that they can become triumphant, people won't even try because folks need to know they can succeed. Teens may wear a mask of "I can't do it," but experience has shown me that it's usually more of a defense mechanism to shield their fear of trying and possibly failing. Addressing the core issue of self-doubt and providing unwavering encouragement are the keys to fostering teen success.

2

If You Build It, They Will Come
Teaching Teens to Craft a Vision

It was quiet in my room. Library quiet. As I well knew, a portion of my students came from families where six or more people might be sharing a two-bedroom home, which meant that a quiet place to read, study, or do homework did not exist for them once they left school. This is why I knew that if I was ever going to create a legitimate means by which my students would become real book readers, the first place I'd have to start was through the creation of a time, space, and place where they could actually read while having the activity of book reading modeled for them by both me, at the front of the room, and their peers, while each student read quietly around the class. Sometimes I used traditional SSR (silent sustained reading), sometimes I utilized a version of DEAR (goodness, it's fun to shout at a bunch of teens, "drop everything and read!" as if they were the lucky millionth customers of my classroom), and sometimes I just provided a chunk of read-our-class-book-now space because of how important it is to give my students time to plow through the pages I ask them to read. Basically, in my own teacher brain, all of these activities fall under the same roof as *Readin' Time*.

And whenever we went into Readin' Time during English class, my students knew I meant business. Even the slightest chitter-chatter between two kids could be enough to throw as many as 35 other readers off. As the conductor of this silent, thoughtful symphony, I knew it was my job to make absolutely sure that disturbances didn't happen. Get comfortable, chill out on the floor if you'd like, but no talking.

"Put it away, Cyndy," I said. "And quickly, too, before I take your cellie and do something like call Thailand to order a pizza." Cyndy scurried to close the phone she'd been secretly fiddling with in her lap underneath her desk. "It's Readin' Time," I reminded her.

"But I was reading," she answered. "Reading a text."

"Yeah, well, do us both a favor and read the text by Mark Twain, okay?" I responded, trying to be witty.

"Look, Mr. Alan, no offense," Cyndy began, "but Mark Twain sucks." Cyndy rolled her eyes, the class laughed, and more than a few of the kids nodded their heads in agreement.

Now, when students roast my favorite authors, it's hard not to take the matter personally. However, a bigger picture had emerged for me. As a teacher I was being offered a front-row seat to the fact that we as a nation were undoubtedly raising a generation of nonbook readers, and though it makes me sound like an old coot to say this, these kids today, with their dang technology, dang self-absorption, and double-dang attitudes of disregard for the value of books . . . well, it's as if Gutenberg never lived.

And the consequences are dire.

Of course, I have to concede that today's kids are reading all the time. Maybe even more than ever. That's because kids today are Screen-Agers (i.e., teens reading screens). However, from my vantage point as an English teacher, I easily recognized that when students read text messages, they weren't using the imaginative, focused, critical-thinking skills that make reading so good for kids' brains. From developmental health professionals to pediatricians to the U.S. Department of Education to the International Reading Association and on and on and on, basically a library's worth of research exists that unequivocally proved that reading was essential to the well-being of kids.

And reading poorly spelled, punctuation-free, profanity-speckled phone type from a homegirl ditching math class was not, I knew, the same as book reading.

This type of reading, as I went on to explain to Cyndy as well as the rest of my students, was more like eating Doritos for dinner. Sure, a person could claim it was food, but Doritos lacked vital nutrition and if salty chips were all a kid ate for sustenance, her health was most assuredly going to suffer.

Same with a teenager's brain, I told them.

Now admittedly, I am a huge fan of technology and a strong advocate for digital literacy, but as a teacher I see my job as one of developing critical thinkers, and clearly, reading text messages was in no way equivalent to reading a novel by one of the greatest authors in American history. Simply put, they are not interchangeable types of reading that similarly empower me to reach my educational goals.

Not that Cyndy wouldn't have liked to debate the point, though.

Yet still, how was I supposed to get my students away from the "Mark Twain sucks" mind-set? Telling teens things like, "Mark Twain is good for you," was almost a surefire recipe for disaster. I'd have more luck trying to prevent them from making out in the halls by decrying the transfer of dangerous oral bacteria. On the other hand, I had a language arts curriculum to get through.

And in order to do so, I needed my kids to be reading the darn books!

All of this got me thinking about the books in my own life, the ones that had really shaped me and made me the type of person I'd become. "Who would I be," I wondered, "if I had not read any books?"

Goodness, I couldn't even imagine it. Yet, shocking as this may sound, I was teaching kids in high school who honestly admitted to me they had made it this far in school without ever having read an entire book. No exaggeration. I have bunches of them every year who come to my class *having never read a book!* (And some of these kids have C and B averages, too, not just a sea of Fs on their report cards.) I mean, some books were so intertwined with my own being that to take them away from the bank of my human experience would be to, most probably, alter the shape and character of the person I had become.

And many adults, I venture to say, feel exactly same way.

Quick activity: List your top two or three favorite books of all time, and then X them out, as if you had never read them. Ask yourself, "Who would I be if I had never read these works?" For me, I can say without reservation that I just don't know. From Dr. Seuss to Victor Hugo to the Bible to Walter Dean Myers, it's almost impossible to imagine who I'd be without having read these texts. Truly, the only thing I do know is that I'd be much worse off as a human being. You too?

The more I thought about all of this, the more I realized how tremendous the positive impact of just one really good book could be to the lives of my students. Especially for kids who had no reservation whatsoever about letting people like me know about their blatant disdain for reading. This is when I decided to create a private selection of books and lesson plans that I would use in my class; books I *knew* would hook my kids and become a slam dunk for classroom instruction.

The creation of a series of titles, the development of a bank of novels that would win over even the most fickle of teenagers, excited me. Why? Because it meant that I would have to read a heck of a lot of new books. (Of course I know admitting this makes me an instant dork. I mean who, in this day and age, gets excited by the prospect of having to spend hours in a library in order to jump in bed early on a Saturday night with nothing more than a reading light, a stack of novels, and a few good pillows to prop up his head? *As a matter of fact, often the most successful among us, that's who.* But that's a different story.)

As every teacher knows, when you get up in front of a class, you're as much salesperson as you are anything else, so my first rule of thumb became to sell to my students only those books about which I, myself, felt authentic passion. Heck, I knew I'd have to be working as hard as any ice representative in PolarBearVille, Alaska, anyway, to get my kids to read, so "personal love of the text" became my cardinal tenet. If I didn't genuinely like it, I didn't genuinely push it. (*Note:* I did plan to open up my classroom reading selections to books my students would—I hoped—one day discover on their own once I converted them into readers, but at the start I made sure that I began with books that I myself loved.)

Rule 1 for Teaching Literature to Reluctant Readers: Choose Books That You Yourself Adore

---

Accessibility became the next criteria for selection. Part of the problem, I realized, with teaching novels by authors like Mark Twain was that my students didn't yet have the literary skills to navigate the works. For kids who hated reading, comprehended material at multiple grade levels below their current placement in school, and had little to no desire to intellectually wrangle with narrative text. Starting off with authors from the mid-1800s, I realized, wasn't my most prudent course of action. Finding contemporary books where my kids would see their own lives directly reflected on the page thus became paramount. Let the powers that be in the world of language arts instruction call me a heretic, I figured. I shelved the classics in favor of novels written much more recently because in my heart I knew that I could eventually do a heck of a lot more teaching with a Walter Dean Myers book that my students would read than an Emily Brontë book that they wouldn't.

> **" I knew that I could eventually do a heck of a lot more teaching with a Walter Dean Myers book that my students would read than an Emily Brontë book that they wouldn't.**

Rule 2 for Teaching Literature to Reluctant Readers: Choose Books in Which Students See Their Own Lives, Their Own Circumstances, and Their Own Vernaculars Directly Reflected on the Page

Finally, I created a third rule for my book choices: make sure that the students whose butts were sitting in the chairs of my classroom would be electrified by the story. Or terrified. Or horrified. Just some kind of -ified as soon as their fingers turned to page 1. Boring was out, thrilling was in, and doing things like dissecting thematic nuances was shelved (at least at the start) for more important matters like uproarious belly laughs. Or scandalous drug abuse. Or freak-you-out terror. (Or peer pressure, sports, drunken driving, gangs, or family dysfunction.) Choosing subject matter in contemporary young adult novels that would get the juices of my students flowing right at the start became of spectacular importance. It was a no-brainer to me that books that required 50 pages of leeway before the plot turned intriguing would be novels I might as well start using as doorstops because my students would never cut these books that much slack. And what could I do? The fact is many of them would simply take a failing grade before slogging through pages they considered boring. When you have no leverage, you have no leverage.

> **Rule 3 for Teaching Literature to Reluctant Readers: Choose Books That Captivate the Interest of Kids the Moment They Read the Back Cover**

Then, by using the excitement that these contemporary authors brought to the page, I started classroom discussions.

There was no grading. Yet.

There were no judgments. Yet.

There were no quizzes, bubble sheets, essay responses, nor evaluations of any sort.

Yet.

First, we simply talked.

The reason I did this was to break the practically Pavlovian model that currently exists in our schools for kids (i.e., Read, test. Read, test. Read, test.). Well, no wonder so many of my students hated reading; their primary association with the activity was that they'd be tested on what they had just read, with a test that would, mind you, often reveal an academic underperformance that would then make my students feel ashamed of themselves.

Maybe it wasn't even the books they hated. Maybe it was just the tests. (And the feelings of low self-esteem they often derived as by-products of scoring so poorly on them.) I mean, it felt like every time we folks in schools asked our students to read, it was because we wanted to examine their comprehension skills about what they had just intellectually digested as if the ultimate point to their reading was for them to provide verifiable data that could be quantified into statistical pie charts for some desk monkey in the state capitol to disaggregate.

Nonsense!

What I needed to do was reframe my students' perceptions in order to get them to realize that the point of reading novels was, first and foremost, to enjoy a delicious story. After all, authors don't pen books in order to have taskmasters illuminate the secret subtexts to be found in thematic literary analysis. Writers write novels to spin good yarns, and if they fail in this capacity, they pretty much fail at the endeavor on the whole. Therefore, when it came to kids who had low skills and an even lower regard for

books and their importance, everything else, I reasoned, would have to fall in line behind illuminating the apparently lost point in our school system that reading books is meant to be, before anything else, enjoyable.

Yep, discovering the pleasure of reading novels would be my strategy. Then we'd hone our language arts skills. Anything else, as I saw it, was putting the cart before the horse.

And really, how hard is it to get teenagers to talk?

"Who in this room has a parent that you feel is unfair, hypocritical, or just totally lame?" I asked.

Hands shot up across the room.

"Who in here has ever felt like the loneliest person on the planet despite the fact you were walking down the halls of a school side by side with thousands of other teenagers at the very same moment?"

Heads bobbed in complete understanding.

"Is there anyone in this room who has not been offered drugs?"

Almost every teenager in every class I have ever taught knew exactly where I was coming from with that one.

Amazingly, through the simple art of tying questions like these to the books I had selected, it took no time at all before we were elbow deep in literary analysis. How? Because good books lead to good talks.

See, that's the thing about great stories: people enjoy knowing more about them even after the story is over. Much like exiting a good movie always leaves the audience talking about the film on the way back to their cars, I knew that reading a good book would leave my students wanting to spend time discussing the events of the novels. The people in the novels. The tricky situations in the novels. Our conversations became our mode of exploring our books so that we could more deeply understand, appreciate, and connect with them.

For regular folks, it's called natural and thoughtful chat. In academic jargon, it's called introductory literary analysis. Plot, character, setting, tone—all of these conversations (and more) soon took place with a host of engaged students because they were taking place in an organic, nonthreatening way through books my kids enjoyed reading.

I then explained to my students that we were going to view English class much like a puppet show. First, we would sit out in the audience and enjoy the performance. Forget the tests. Forget the exams. Forget all the school stuff they'd spent years building up a resistance to. To pinch a line from the motto of the Oakland Raiders, I told them, "Just read, baby. Just read."

But then, I informed my class, we would take a peek behind the curtain, too, so that we could see how the puppeteer pulled the strings, made the characters dance, and crafted the exciting and thoughtful elements of the show.

My list of books took years to grow and eventually came to include a range of intriguing, disparate novels. Some were short and spicy. Others were long and meaty. Some were famous, some obscure, some were hailed, and some were banned. *Note:* Choosing books off the lists of banned books always made for a great selling point to my students. After all, what teens don't love doing things that adults tell them not to? The only thing each of these novels had in common was that my kids greatly enjoyed them. (See Appendix G, "No-Fail Books for Teens.")

What I found was that there were definitely books out there that would most assuredly gain the approval of teenagers—even teenage boys of color, the hardest-to-reach demographic in the world of both literature and school. The myth was not true: kids *would* read. I simply needed to meet them at the point where their interests lay and then build meaningful, relevant, accessible connections.

Did it help that I was unyielding in my belief that there is no such thing as an unreachable or unteachable kid? Most assuredly. And truth be told, soon enough the students in my class were filling their mental gas tanks with books in a way they never had before. All it took was the right selection, a bit of salesmanship, and a whole lot of belief in what the power of reading could mean to the life of a teen.

After all, some books change lives.

Teach Teens to Craft a Vision

It's no *duh* that having a personal vision about the things I could accomplish with teens as both an educator and a writer has played a huge role in my journey toward successfully reaching kids. But how often do we invite our teens to conceptualize and then actualize a vision for themselves? Sadly, I discovered what happens when kids lack vision and purpose with a student named TiJuan as he blazed a fiery path to teenage calamity.

Before a person becomes a teacher, he usually envisions himself being a patient, compassionate, and forever reasonable professional. Then you get students in your class like TiJuan and find yourself behaving like a reality TV show contestant. Goodness knows I'll never forget the day I completely lost it with a tenth grader over the inane choices he was so obviously making with his life.

"Dude, you're fifteen, you don't do a lick of homework, ya ditch school all the time, and you speak to me like I'm the one who's got the problem in this relationship. I mean, how come I seem to be caring more about your freakin' future than you do?"

I was hot. And I expected an answer. I'd cut this kid every damn break in the book and still he was refusing to step up to do the things he needed to do in order to be successful either in my class or in life.

"Cuz I already know my future," TiJuan answered. But he replied with a softness, a lack of ferocity and battle that caught me completely off guard. I'd expected confrontational hostility. Instead I got demoralized resignation. In just a few words TiJuan had clearly communicated to me his expectation

> As a teacher, I know that how teenagers see themselves and where they see themselves play a humongous role in where they will eventually find themselves later in life.

for a future characterized by despondency—as if poverty, violence, shame, and a life full of misery were already foregone conclusions for him.

And then he looked at me with sad eyes—eyes that held a glimmer of hope—as if somehow there was something I could say that would possibly be the one right thing that would change for him what seemed like a preordained destiny.

I gave it my best. I was inspirational, encouraging, filled with passion and vigor and all sorts of deep, meaningful advice about how "it is never over till it is over" and how "this moment right here could be the turning point of [his] life" and on and on. Being the softie that I am, tears even came to my eyes. And tough as he appeared on the outside with his baggy clothes and cornrows in his hair, TiJuan struggled to hold back tears of his own. I made the best effort I could to get through.

But I didn't.

TiJuan ended up dropping out of school and fathering a baby at the age of 17. The last I heard, he had a tattoo on his neck and was being "looked for" by some people.

On the other hand, I once had a student named Monica, a blonde girl in my tenth-grade English class back when I taught at a private school on the West Side of Los Angeles. For Monica's first big essay that year, she turned in a neatly typed assignment inside a blue folder. A really nice blue folder. Not one of those 49-cent jobs from Target but a totally sweet, executive-style, textured plastic folder that must have cost about 6 bucks.

"Whoa," I said when she handed it to me. "Nice folder, Monica. But a bit of overkill, don't you think?"

"Nothing but the best, Mr. Alan," she replied. "Nothing but the best." Monica then sat back down in her chair, straightened her spine, and waited for the world to unfold before her.

And everyone in class knew it would.

In just a few words, it was quite clear that Monica planned on college, graduate school, high-powered employment, a fat salary, a sweet house, luxury cars in her driveway, and, for all I knew, her own Hawaiian island.

Two kids. Both 15. Both living in the same city, less than 10 miles apart, yet entire planets away from one another when it came to the visions they held for their own respective futures.

These two students exemplify how there is simply no way to underestimate the value of vision and expectations to the life of a teen. As a teacher, I know that how teenagers see themselves and where they see themselves play a humongous role in where they will eventually find themselves later in life.

And the correlation deviates little.

Now, do money, parents, environment, school, social class, and so forth also play a role? Absolutely. However, in a teenager's life, these elements are just pieces to the puzzle, not the entire puzzle itself. Sure, Monica was a rich white kid, but nobody made her go over and above in a quest to be outstanding in the way that she did. (Trust me, there are plenty of rich white kids who don't do squat.) And while TiJuan was a poor, half-black, half-Hispanic kid, nobody was making him ditch class, cause trouble, and flunk out of school. (Trust me on this one, too; there are plenty of students of color going far and above to earn a solid education despite tremendous obstacles.)

The heart of the difference lies in the prisms through which each of these teens saw themselves . . . and the potential of their future.

Maybe more than any other group of people on this planet, teenagers are at a stage of life where they are perpetually operating under self-fulfilling prophesies. Kids who see failure, violence, and poverty in their future eventually find it, much like kids who see accomplishment, accolades, and highly compensated employment in their future typically find a form of that as well. What often matters so much to teens—which also happens to be something that we are doing an absolutely terrible job of teaching to today's students (I mean, it's absolutely nowhere in the national conversation we perpetually have about the direction of our schools' curricula)—is that the inner vision teenagers hold for themselves will dictate more about their future than any standardized, fill-in-the-bubble, multiple-choice test they will ever take.

Ever.

As an educator, I know it's not a coincidence that teens who are in the top 10 percent of their class very often have the clearest, most positive, most hopeful inner visions for themselves of all the students in the school—and that the other 90 percent of kids all too often have very little or no vision for who they can be, for what they can be, or for how they can be it. At best they're often fuzzy about this type of conversation. At worst they tell me they have never even thought about it and don't want to think about it now; then they tell me, "Shove off, I have plenty of time to think about that stupid kind of stuff" (except their language frequently has a bit more salt to it). And as we see time after time after time, this lack of inner vision far too often ends up sabotaging teens in harsh and unpredictable ways with dire consequences.

We must recognize that a teen without a personal vision is a teen without the most fundamental tool a person needs in this world to eventually succeed. Abraham Lincoln had a vision. Martin Luther King had a vision. The landlord who owns three apartment complexes down the street also had a vision. Teens need to be taught the supreme importance of how their own inner vision ultimately becomes the foremost instrument that will steer the direction of their life. Otherwise, their existence too often resembles a rudderless ship.

Tips for Teaching Teens to Craft a Vision

Explain the Importance of Crafting a Vision

Look, no one gets into a car and starts to drive without a destination in mind. Same with life. To arrive anywhere worthwhile, teenagers need a sense of where they want to go.

As I tell my kids often, the life of a teen is very much like an open, fertile patch of land. They can plant rose bushes, they can grow tomatoes, they can cultivate chrysanthemums. Truly, they should plant what they want. However, the mistake far too many teens make is thinking that if they don't plant anything, nothing will grow. That's where they are wrong. As anyone who gardens knows, if you don't work the soil and tend to your plot of land, you'll get weeds. And not *that* kind of weed, as I like to joke. I'm talking about unwanted, wild plants that take deep root, spoil the habitat, and often take immense effort to uproot, remove, and replace.

This is not my rule; it's the rule of Mother Nature. Teens *must* craft a vision.

Allow Teens to Craft Their Own Vision

All teens have ambition—yep, even those sittin'-on-the-couch-eatin'-potato-chips teens who wouldn't change their socks if mold started to grow on their feet. But how often are teenagers earnestly asked to think about their own desires, to brainstorm their own goals, to weigh their own biggest interests, and to speculate about the type of fulfilling future they'd most prefer to live if they could be and do anything that they wanted?

The answer is not very often—and hardly ever in our contemporary middle and high school curricula, which most certainly explains a great deal of the academic disengagement. We're blindly asking kids to learn skills in a vacuum with the faith that one day the things we are teaching will have value to them. "Uh, yeah right," they're saying.

Challenge teens as to how they see themselves, ask teens how they wish to express themselves, and assist teens in exploring expanded options for themselves.

Then listen. We're all given two ears and one mouth, but all too often adults, at least when they converse with teenagers, have the ratio completely backward.

Encourage Meaningfulness

People whine all the time about how today's teens don't have any sense of motivation, but I have kids who will sleep on a concrete sidewalk in a rainstorm for hot concert tickets. Trust me, today's teens are motivated. Highly motivated. That's if they are asked to pursue goals they find meaningful. Objectives that have deep, internal, personal value to teens trigger in them a desire to give an effort filled with *oomph* (and *oomph* is always necessary to achieve anything worthwhile in this world). Ask teens to reach for the stars, go for the gold, chase the pot of riches at the end of the rainbow (or any other cliché you can think of). But just remember to make sure that it's their stars, their gold, their pot of riches you are encouraging them to pursue, because teens respond best when they have meaningful goals of authentic, personal value.

I can't be more emphatic about this point: meaningfulness is an essential, underlying ingredient to exceptional teen performance.

Watch for the Three Enemies of Crafting a Vision

Not Being Specific

Teens are often vague. Ask them how they are, and they'll tell you, "Fine." Ask them how something tastes, and they'll say, "Good." But what they often don't realize is that when it comes to crafting a personal vision, vagueness hampers goal achievement instead of advancing it. As opposed to having teens say, "I want to get good grades" (an admirable goal), challenge them to specify their aims, such as "I want to earn at least three As on my second-semester report card with another B+ in one other class." Remember, specificity begets focus, and focus begets clear vision.

Becoming Impatient

Teens want results now. Heck, in a wi-fi, hip-hop world, if an Internet page even dares to take more than a few seconds to load, teens will click off to a new website in a nanosecond, which means that asking them to have faith that the seeds they are sowing in these early years of their lives are going to pay valuable dividends in their later years strikes them as a philosophy that comes straight from the times when mankind wore loincloths and didn't yet have iTunes. (The old days are all the same to them.) Sure, patience might be the antithesis of a teen's modern technological expectations, but human beings take time to develop. And they make mistakes along the way. And they grow at a pace more aligned with Mother Nature than Father Semiconductor. Illuminate the pitfalls of impatience, a quality that all too frequently sabotages many teens who are on the right track.

Letting Others Pull You Down

The fact of the matter is that teens' friends and peers hold the greatest sway over their day-to-day behaviors. And teens will unfortunately traverse very foolish roads and go down with many sinking ships just so that they don't look bad in front of their buddies. This is why it is critical to illuminate the need for teens to hang out with other teens who will tell them not to jump off the bridge even though everyone else is doing it. (Yes, such kids exist.) Encourage teens to "kick it" with other teens who have positive personal visions for themselves. It's rough out there for today's teenagers, and when times get tough and the big decisions come up, they are often going to turn to their friends.

The Principle of Classroom Osmosis

Teaching Teens to Tend to Their 'Tude

The famous French writer Voltaire once said, "Common sense is not so common," and if being a teacher has taught me anything, it's that nowhere is this phrase more true than in our schools. When it came to getting my students to read books, I had learned through firsthand experience that the foremost obstacle was not that my kids were reluctant readers; it was that all people are reluctant readers . . . until the right book comes along. Yes, Mark Twain bombed, but I discovered that Walter Dean Myers would sail. Dickens fell flat, but Sharon Draper would fly. Jane Austen, Thomas Hardy, and Herman Melville were practically DOA (dead on arrival), but S. E. Hinton, Laurie Halse Anderson, and Orson Scott Card had wings on which my classes could soar.

I also had to admit that the same logic about what constituted a reluctant reader applied to everyone. For example, I like to consider myself a voracious reader, but if someone slipped an organic chemistry textbook under my nose and told me to open to Chapter 12, it wouldn't be too long before I'd start uttering phrases such as "I don't get it" and "This is stupid" and "Why do I have to read this?"

The exact words that millions of teachers like me have heard spoken from the mouths of our students many, many times over. While the right book could keep almost anyone awake, the wrong book could put almost anyone to sleep.

And me, I snore, flail my arms, and drool on my pillow. A bad book can be an ugly thing.

My job wasn't to tell my students what they were supposed to like and appreciate. My job, as I saw it, was to understand what they liked and appreciated and then use it as the springboard from which I could build meaningful, academically enriching connections to a widened path of intellectual material.

And why? Because literacy had clearly become the passport to success in the twenty-first century and those students, not just in America but across the globe, who did not possess the ability to read and write with marked proficiency would most likely find themselves excluded more and more from a workforce (and an upper social echelon) that valued thinkers over laborers. Yes, America had always rewarded brains over brawn, but ever since the ball dropped in Times Square marking our passage into the new millennium, the gulf between those who worked with their minds and those who worked with their hands had grown to almost Grand Canyon–size proportions. My kids, as I could clearly see, *needed* to know how to read and write. And well!

The only real question was how.

I already had an advantage many other teachers weren't enjoying: my kids were actually reading books (which most certainly makes the task of teaching language arts skills much easier). Next, I had to pay heed to the fact that my students, contrary to popular belief, liked to be challenged. And my students, contrary to popular belief, liked to be pushed. And my students, contrary to popular belief, liked to work.

What I needed, though, was common ground between the two masters I was seeking to serve. If I could figure out a way to make the academic classroom objectives my school district had hired me to teach feed into and harmonize with the natural energy and excitement of my students—a big if—there might be a way to accomplish both.

The only possible way to do this was to think differently about the instructional goals I was supposed to address while being willing not to use materials just because they had been given to me by a department chairperson or a vice principal. My classroom needed my voice, and no one else was going to be able to provide me with that. It was something I would have to seek and find for myself.

A famous quote says, "If you want different answers, ask different questions," so I did. Maybe the problem wasn't with the students at all. Maybe the problem was with the methodology by which I was delivering the subject matter.

I decided to reconceptualize my approach to delivering the curriculum and began to lean much more heavily on project-based learning.

My school's barometer for measuring students' comprehension of literary elements like characterization was whether they marked the correct bubble on some interminably boring standardized test. To best teach my students this area of the language arts, I decided to have them write their own original classroom plays, after reading texts like George Bernard Shaw's *Pygmalion* and August Wilson's *Fences* in order to understand the machinations of character as well as plot, setting, tone, dramatic conflict, and historical context, along with the relationship of these elements to each other. Students wore costumes, brought in strobe lights, and laid down soundtracks. They didn't just learn about characters on a stagnant page; they dynamically became them in flesh and blood, with me believing in my heart that by the time the bubble-sheet tests came down the pipeline, my kids would have the literary elements they needed to know down cold.

My school's idea of exposing my students to a diversity of world literature was to have them read one or two short stories from flavorless—and incredibly expensive—world literature textbooks designed to be nauseatingly politically correct. For my unit on South Africa and apartheid, I chose instead to have my students read meaty books like *Kaffir Boy* by Mark Mathabane and *The Power of One* by Bryce Courtenay and then break off into cooperative learning groups: they became travel agents who delivered digital slide presentations that sought to sell international vacation packages to other members of the class in order for all of us to learn about the culture, economy, climate, ethnicity, history of the government, and effect of setting on the outlook and circumstances of the people. The cruelty of racism, as my kids clearly saw, knew no international boundaries, and the connections flowed and flowed, from Johannesburg to the Jim Crow era to *Brown v. the Board of Education* to Hurricane Katrina to their own lives as teenagers being followed by undercover security nearly every time they went into a department store because of the color of their skin or the way they dressed.

We debated the legalization of marijuana before writing the traditional compare-and-contrast essay (I discovered that some of my students who openly admitted to smoking pot were very much against the legalization of marijuana because of the negative impact it might have on society in terms of being a gateway drug to harder substance abuse as well as potentially putting more intoxicated drivers on the roads). We analyzed propaganda through a dissection of news media to gain an understanding of what constituted veracity in the age of Internet news. We performed spoken-word poetry in two- and three-voice poems. We even read Shakespeare's longest play, *Hamlet,* as the culmination of our drama study. Basically, we wrote, wrote, wrote, talked, talked, talked, and read, read, read about subject matters that were of major interest to them. (And yes, Shakespeare was most definitely of major interest to my students once I turned on the lightbulb illuminating his unparalleled and brilliant insights into human nature.) Basically, we read more books during the course of one school year than most of my kids had read in their entire lives prior to my class, worked our tails off (e.g., groups of my students meeting on Sundays to get all their work done for Monday presentations was not uncommon at all), and smiled a heck of a lot as we did so. And if there was one thing that became the secret wellspring from which I concocted all of my far-reaching educational ideas, it was that I started opening my ears more and more to listen to my kids.

Truthfully, they taught me more about how to teach them than any textbook, college class, professional developer, or school administrator ever could.

What I had discovered through being a simple listener was a means by which I could raise the level of my own classroom practice so that my students could experience tangible, data-driven, get-you-a-diploma-and-then-get-you-into-college type of success while at the same time having a heck of a good time learning in their English class. Even students who were failing multiple other high school courses would boast to me, "You know, Mr. Alan, this is the only class that I don't ditch."

"I'm flattered," I'd reply dryly.

As I began to see, the philosophy of marrying authentically engaging material to standards-based curricular rigor and high expectations was paying excellent dividends. (See Figure 3–1.)

As a teacher, when your kids are in the groove, it leaves you feeling really good about the world. (That's just the way we teachers are wired.) But being a teacher, in my opinion, was about more than just doing well during my between-the-bells workday. It also meant getting involved around campus in extracurricular activities. In a school as large as ours, a variety of opportunities existed, and several intrigued me. AVID leapt to mind first.

Figure 3.1　California High School Exit Exam Data

	Year Tested 2004	Year Tested 2005	Year Tested 2006	Year Tested 2007
Grouping	**10th Grade**	**10th Grade**	**10th Grade**	**10th Grade**
Lynwood High School English Language Arts Pass Rate	59%	63%	59%	60%
Lynwood High School Mathematics Pass Rate	50%	49%	53%	49%
Alan Sitomer's English Language Arts Classes Pass Rate	**96%**	**98%**	**95%**	**96%**
Centennial High School English Language Arts Pass Rate	49%	50%	55%	60%
Hollywood High School English Language Arts Pass Rate	63%	63%	58%	69%
Pasadena High School English Language Arts Pass Rate	72%	77%	80%	77%
Santa Monica High School English Language Arts Pass Rate	90%	89%	89%	90%
Entire State of California English Language Arts Pass Rate	75%	76%	77%	77%

*All information is based upon data collected through the California Department of Education, Lynwood High School, and UCLA's Institute for Democracy, Education, and Access

AVID is a nationally renowned educational program whose name derives from an acronym: Advancement Via Individual Determination. Essentially, AVID targets students in the academic middle—B, C, and D students—who have the desire and willingness to work hard so that they can go to college. Typically, they are the first in their families to attend a university and many of them are from low-income or minority families.

I took on the role of Lynwood High School's very first senior class AVID teacher, and I'm proud to say that 100 percent of my students ended up graduating from high school and going on to college, a remarkable feat, considering that they entered Lynwood High as freshmen in a class of approximately 1,550, of which only about 875 graduated. (*Note:* Urban schools such as the one where I teach consistently post at least a 40 percent nongraduation rate [Landsberg 2006]). I'd say "dropout rate," but schools like mine insist on pointing out that some kids end up transferring to other high schools without telling us where they're going, and since we can't track them, we don't want to take the blame for their not earning their diplomas. Nationwide, it makes stats in this area very murky.

Needless to say, I was exceptionally proud of my AVID seniors, and without a doubt, becoming an AVID teacher made me both a better educator and a better person. Really, I couldn't be more enthusiastic about my thumbs-up for AVID (if you're interested in learning more about what an AVID teacher does, how the program works, or how you can bring AVID to your school— it's a national program—go to its website at www.avidonline.org).

I also became our school's mock trial coach, taking on the job of helming our high school's moot court legal team. Though the workload was gigantic (I remember one stretch where I was on campus working with my team seven Sundays in a row, preparing for trial), our team enjoyed a few special afternoons down at the Los Angeles County Courthouse, where our kids beat the pants off a few private high schools populated by rich, white kids with every seeming advantage. My students would show up in ill-fitting shirts and mismatched polyester ties and face down students wearing DKNY jackets and Kenneth Cole black leather shoes . . . and then proceed to take them out to the woodshed intellectually. We never won it all—Los Angeles is a big county, one of the largest in the United States— but we came close on a few occasions, with my students shattering a whole lot of stereotypes all along the way. Hard work, preparation, and belief in ourselves became the pillars of Lynwood High School's mock trial program and the truth was, all of us took great joy in proving that notorious Lynwood possessed the intellectual ability to field such a competitive high school legal team.

I also taught a creative writing course, helped extend community outreach, and constantly sought ways to build bridges for my students to opportunities that existed for them in the world beyond Lynwood's confines. One thing I learned as an inner-city teacher is that for many of my kids, their worldview ended at the boundaries of our city. Me, I've been to Europe, Asia, Central America, Mexico, and Canada. Bunches of my students have never even flown on an airplane before.

Yet, no matter what I did around my high school, it never felt like enough. There was always so much more a teacher could do. Additionally, as I was starting to learn, when it came to some of the happenings in America's classrooms, things could get downright ugly.

It's almost laughable all the stuff they don't tell you when you accept a teaching position. I walked into my classroom as an educator prepared to instruct my students in things such as making subjects and verbs agree, writing the five-paragraph essay, and dissecting novels like *Animal Farm*. Nothing prepared me, however, to deal with kids who had been sexually molested, victimized by gang violence, or abused and abandoned by their biological parents.

Before I came to Lynwood, I had always thought I'd make my biggest mark by improving student academic performance. However, now I know that if I have made a meaningful contribution at all, it's been to the lives of real, individual people, kids that our society, to one degree or another, has let down.

For certain, I know the mark my students have left on me is indelible. Autumn was one such young lady.

Autumn was an A student. Bright. Outgoing. Sat in the front row of class with a smile on her face every day. How could I ever forget the afternoon she came to me and confided that she had been sexually abused? By her uncle, a man who (get this) drove an ice-cream truck for a living. I could hardly believe my ears.

Actually, Autumn's abuse, I discovered, had happened years earlier when she was only 9 years old. However, like many childhood victims, she had never told anyone. Neither, as it turned out, had any of her three younger sisters. It was a family secret that each of them had kept from one another their entire lives.

One evening, though, when the youngest girl in the family winced in pain when she went to sit on a stool at a pizza parlor, Autumn flashed back to a time when she was her sibling's age and grew suspicious about the cause of her sister's anguish. Later that evening, Autumn confronted her youngest sister, and soon all four girls in the family had a conference and realized that they'd all gone through the very same horrible experience but had never mentioned it to one another.

Once Autumn informed me of the situation, I helped her understand my obligation to alert the proper authorities. I explained that referring the matter to the right department would not be a betrayal of her trust in me, but rather a move toward something of supreme and immediate importance: this guy had to be stopped!

I knew that in her heart, Autumn felt scared. However, in her heart, Autumn also knew that she was standing at the doorstep of an opportunity to prevent this horror from ever happening to goodness knows how many other young girls, including her own younger cousins.

I wasn't present at the family conference when the news was broken to Autumn's parents—a social worker was—but from what Autumn told me, the situation was tense. Autumn's mother didn't want to admit that her brother could be such a monster, but, as it turned out, she'd "had a feeling about something fishy" for quite some time but never acted upon it, preferring to choose the route of denial and avoidance instead. And her children paid the price.

Autumn's father wanted to kill his brother-in-law. Literally murder him. Autumn told me her dad was fully prepared to take justice into his own hands, murder his brother-in-law, and then serve out the rest of his life in prison with no regrets whatsoever.

From what I know, it worked out like this. Autumn's uncle was arrested by the police. Autumn's family went into counseling. Soon thereafter, Autumn's family moved to another part of the city, with all of the girls switching schools in the process. I never really found out too much more because, though I had hoped to stay in touch, when you teach as many students as I do per year, many of them, once they are gone from your life, are gone forever. Transience for the children of the working poor in our country is a very common problem, especially in the Latino community, and kids float in and out of my life at an alarming rate, almost like stories in progress that I very often never get to see finished.

The only other thing I ever heard about it came two years later when a former student of mine walked in one day and told me that Autumn ("You remember her, don't you Mr. Alan?" How could I ever forget?) had graduated high school, was currently enrolled in community college, and said, "Hi."

"Hi." That's all I got. Still, it was good enough. Plenty, as a matter of fact.

However, I have to admit that deep down, I still hold fears about the fateful day when a children's ice-cream truck driver will storm into my classroom, wielding a rainbow bomb pop and a sawed-off shotgun, blaming me for the hellish turn of events his own life took, and start firing away.

Maybe that sounds funny, but it's not a joke. The truth is, my experience with Autumn sent me reeling.

Though I want to protect all my students, I had to face up to the fact that no matter what I did, I couldn't. Though I want to empower all my kids, I had to face up to the fact that my aims were idealistic and naïve. Though I want to hoist all my students out of poverty, lift them out of a culture of violence, move them beyond a community plagued by gangs, guns, and drugs, I had to face a blunt and cold reality: it was just flat-out unrealistic for me to accomplish 100 percent of these goals. Kids would be victimized. Kids would slip through the cracks. Kids would be beaten, abandoned, and abused.

I couldn't save them all.

Though I had been at my job for years at this point, this realization came quite suddenly to me. And immediately I became morose. I started to swing back and forth, enjoying the highest of highs with some kids and the lowest of lows with others. Like I said, no matter how much I did, there was always more to do; my efforts were never enough. Students got into Stanford. Students got shot. Students raised their SAT scores. Students got pregnant. My inner psychological balance swayed like a flag in hurricane-force winds. At the exact moment I was ready to quit teaching because the emotional taxation of being an educator was just way too much to take anymore, inevitably, some of my students would prance into my room with a magical twinkle in their eyes, sharing news so positive it would zap me with a bolt of joy.

To mix a few clichés, my cup was running over at the same time that my inner well was running dry. There was no such thing as the status quo. Day after day I witnessed perpetual polarities: chaos and order, pain and beauty, despondency and inspiration.

Finally, I found some solace in a quote I read on a wall in another school; I wrote it down on a napkin, and went home and retyped it.

I've come to the frightening conclusion that I am the decisive element in the classroom. It's my daily mood that makes the weather. As a teacher, I possess a tremendous power to make a child's life miserable or joyous. I can be a tool of torture or an instrument of inspiration. I can humiliate or humor, hurt or heal. In all situations, it is my response that decides whether a crisis will be escalated or de-escalated and a child humanized or de-humanized.

—Dr. Haim Ginott

Basically, I extrapolated from this quote the unique idea that ultimately I, as the teacher in my classroom, was the weather. Not *like* the weather; I *was* the weather. The deeper I looked at this idea, the more I became aware of its tremendous power.

No, I couldn't control all the things that happened outside the four walls of my room. I couldn't control the violence, the mayhem, the insanity, the corruption, the abuse, or the greed. But I could control how I responded to these things. I came to understand that if I was sunny and bright and optimistic and hopeful and tenaciously determined to forge on in spite of all obstacles, my students, as if by osmosis or something, would also become sunny and bright and optimistic and hopeful and tenaciously determined to forge on in spite of all obstacles.

That's when the sunlight began to return.

I also began to think about the fact that these tragedies weren't happening to me; they were happening to my kids. And, out of a misguided attempt to be empathetic, I was becoming glum, when what I needed to do was become more of a pillar of hope to provide solace and strength.

No, I couldn't control the horrors in the community, the inane mandates that came down from above, nor the nasty backbiting that went on in the lunchroom. But I could control the intellectual and emotional climate of my own classroom, and once I understood this—and understood that this was indeed enough—the clouds of despondency began to lift.

Now of course, there are many great educators who put in long, long hours at Lynwood High, in the classrooms, in administration, and at ground zero, the school district. It's not some kind of black-and-white scenario where one miracle worker can come in and save the day on our campus. This is why I detest the way that Hollywood portrays my profession, as if all it takes is one great savior educator (usually a cute, thin, suburban white girl) to rescue all the kids from their own inevitable demise. Sure, it may sell movie tickets, but this is a preposterous oversimplification of how things really work.

Visit any troubled school across the country and you are almost always guaranteed to find honest, hardworking people going over and above in almost superhuman ways to make things better for their students. Heck, I could write a book about the Herculean efforts some of my peers in the Lynwood Unified School District are consistently making toward improving our campus so that it's a better, more productive, safe, and nourishing place.

Yet they get very little love. (However, you'll read about them later in Chapter 7.)

> "
> I came to understand that if I was sunny and bright and optimistic and hopeful and tenaciously determined to forge on in spite of all obstacles, my students, as if by osmosis or something, would also become sunny and bright and optimistic and hopeful and tenaciously determined to forge on in spite of all obstacles.

Yes, Hollywood loves the plot line of the kid with a thousand bad teachers who is brought to the brink of an apocalypse but then, blessed by that one great educator, turns his life around. However, that scenario is fictitiously oversimplified. What real teachers like me are doing out there on the front lines every day is anything but fiction. And none of us is doing it alone. I know I'm not.

Anyway, it was at this point when I became determined to try to be the best teacher I could be regardless of what any others were doing in their classrooms, in the administration offices, in the state capitol, or in Washington, DC, as far as public education was concerned. Despondency, I came to realize, was really just a by-product of my own feelings of victimization. I had fallen prey to bemoaning the things I could not control instead of taking full ownership over the things I could. To be the best educator I could possibly be, I had to embrace the simple fact that attitude was everything.

My attitude.

So I became the weather.

...s me crazy that so many teenagers believe that their attitude is
...thing beyond their control. Or something they are not responsible
for. Or something that they can't do anything about.

It's just not true!

No, teenagers cannot change the color of their skin, the knock of their
knees, or the disproportionate size of their left earlobe (though I've seen
them spend countless hours fretting over similar dilemmas). But teens can
change their attitude—and shift it and mold it and hone it and craft it so
that it one day develops into a finely whetted tool that will empower them
to enjoy a great deal of success in life.

As the sign on my classroom door clearly reads, "Your attitude will
determine your altitude."

Matter of fact, this sign is so important to my way of thinking that I
have it posted in multiple locations around my room. This way, students
can't avoid reading it no matter where they are in my class.

Really, do teens with bad 'tudes ever end up in good places? Do they
win over teachers? Do they give their parents endless reasons to boast and
feel proud? Do they have a stream of friends beating down their doors to
share good times with them?

Of course not.

No matter how you view it, there's a direct relationship between teenagers' attitudes and their eventual performance, whether it be in academics, social life, sports, whatever. Truly, this idea strikes me as a principle
so simple to comprehend, yet so fundamental to assisting teens in reaping
the benefits we all hope they do, that sometimes I am genuinely baffled by
what our school systems require us to teach. I mean, we give all sorts of
math instruction year after year to teens without ever mandating that they
learn one of life's most simple, yet critical mathematical formulas:

a bad attitude ≠ a good result

I call it life math. Here's another lesson I make sure my kids learn:

a good attitude > bad circumstances

The unvarnished truth I've seen played out over and over again with teens is that a good attitude will triumph over brains and talent practically every day of the week. As most educators know, hardworking teens with smiles in their hearts will inevitably surpass the achievements of gifted kids with chips on their shoulders most of the time. It's the classic tortoise-and-hare scenario, a phenomenon I saw exemplified through Diego and Glen.

Diego was named perfectly by his parents. He was bright, good-looking, and spirited, almost dashing in an old-time Hollywood movie sort of way. Diego was smarter than the streets, argumentative about incredibly minute points during class discussion (and most infuriatingly, was right far too often for my liking), and magnetic in a way that caused the knees of girls to melt when he walked down the halls. He could have been anything.

But he became a dropout. In hindsight, I think his cleverness was his downfall because he was so good at avoiding the rules he came to believe that rules did not apply to him. Eventually he got caught up in a deceptive web of his own creation and went from one of the most intelligent kids at our school to a bitter, angry, no-diploma-holding young man who stopped by my class a few years after he'd quit Lynwood wearing a cement mixer's shirt. Not that there's anything wrong with mixing cement for a living . . . unless you don't want to and you've become trapped in the job because of your own crappy attitude about how the world ought to work.

Most assuredly, Diego felt that because he was so gifted and talented and good-looking, the world owed him something.

Bzzzp! Wrong answer, Diego. (And *argghh* . . . so frustrating.)

On the other hand, in Diego's class sat a kid named Glen, who was as mild mannered as a flower child and unfailingly courteous to the point of being annoying. Intellectually, well, let's just say that Glen's coffeepot seemed to be permanently set on lukewarm.

However, Glen did all his homework. And he asked question after question. And he said "please" and "thank you" and sat in the front row of class and worked hard to assimilate feedback into his work and gave his teachers handwritten thank-you cards for Christmas and never missed a day of school and on and on and on. It was virtually impossible not to like Glen. Though his work was consistently mediocre, he chugged and chugged along.

"Mr. Alan," Glen said to me one day during lunch in his senior year, "will you help me with my application essay?"

Though I didn't teach senior English at the time, I had a lot of experience with college application essays and many of my former students came back to me during their senior year to tap me for help. Glen arrived looking for assistance with his application to the University of California at Santa Barbara.

I was shocked. Though I was sure Glen had a decent GPA (grade point average), I knew that getting into UCSB was a highly competitive venture. I'd even had some particularly stellar students get rejected from UCSB in years past. Of course, I didn't say anything to Glen (bursting bubbles is not my style), and I helped him with his essay, but truthfully I didn't think he had much of a chance.

Besides, his essay was poorly executed.

Yet Glen was eager and Glen was courteous and Glen was determined to sharpen his essay to the best of his abilities. So I worked and worked and worked with him until, after four drafts, he finally got it to the point where the essay became solid.

Solidly mediocre.

I mean, it's not like I was going to break the rules and write the dang thing for him myself. Besides, the deadline to apply was approaching and I had gone about as far as I could go with him, considering he wasn't even in my class any longer and I had lots of other kids to teach. Eleven days and four drafts was enough. When Glen mailed it off, I made sure to check that he applied to a broad spectrum of colleges, schools that would be less competitive to get into. Seniors never want to put all their eggs into one basket, and in my heart I doubted very much that Glen would be accepted to the university of his first choice.

I was wrong. Glen was accepted to UCSB. Obviously, the admissions staff had seen something in him that had escaped me. The news jarred me so much that I even went and had a chat with Glen's senior English teacher to ask if she'd heard about Glen's developments.

She was surprised, too. After all, she knew the caliber of candidates for which UCSB was looking. But then she said to me a small phrase with a little laugh that pretty much summed it all up: "Kind of crazy, huh? Yet he does have a great attitude, like the Little Engine That Could."

Diego had it all. Glen had little. But the little Glen had proved to be much, much more when all was said and done.

And isn't that how life works over and over again?

Teach teens about the tremendous importance of attitude. It moves mountains.

● Tips for Teaching Teens to Create Positive Attitudes

Teach Teens to Take Responsibility for Their Attitudes

Teenagers' attitudes are something that they alone control and create, even if they don't recognize this is the case. For example, some kids get offered an entry-level job sweeping floors and view the work as beneath them, while other teens view the same job offer as an opportunity to learn the ropes while putting some cash in their pockets. It's not the job that's different; it's the attitude a teen has toward sweeping the floors that gives the work its real meaning—and pretty clearly forecasts the chances of a kid's success as well.

Teens don't choose their parents, they don't choose their genetic features, and they most certainly don't choose things like the effects of puberty. But teens do choose their own attitudes, and when they take responsibility over this area of their lives, many flowers begin to bloom.

Teach Teens They're Free to Change Their Attitudes at Any Time

It's amazing how many times an attitude shift is the exact remedy teenagers need in order to solve the most vexing issue in their life. What's even more amazing is the fact that many teenagers don't even realize that they are allowed to change their attitudes. Many kids are under the delusion that because they behaved a certain way in the past, they need to behave that same way in the present. However, as I am always showing my students, if the way they behaved in the past isn't bringing them the results they want in the present, then they're going to have to change the way they behave in the present in order to reap different, better results in the future.

Encourage teens to clear out the clutter of the poor attitudes that are causing difficulties for them. As life math says, a bad attitude ≠ a good result.

Tell Teens That a Good Attitude Takes Work

Blame is easy. Excuses are simple. Pointing the finger at someone else and laying faults in another person's lap for things that are not going well in your own life is one of the most uncomplicated and undemanding things a teenager can do.

But accountability, now that's hard. Remaining optimistic in the face of troubles, now that's challenging. Accepting fault when there are problems—wow, now that takes maturity and effort.

The simple fact is that building a good attitude requires hard, perpetual work. The bad news is it's not easy (which I am always honest about). But the good news is that for teens who do the hard work, the results pay off in spades.

● Watch for the Three Enemies of Good Attitudes

Letting Slips Turn Into Snowballs

No one's perfect, and a teen who comes in with a twisted attitude cannot be expected to realign everything and become top of the heap immediately. Therefore, when teens falls off the new attitude horse and slip back into old patterns of detrimental thinking (something to occasionally be expected), they don't need someone ready to blast them for their mistakes but rather someone who has empathy for their plight and knows how to encourage them to get up, dust themselves off, and try again. Remember, the unsuccessful dieter is not the one who slips up and has an ice-cream sundae but rather the one who doesn't return to healthy habits of eating after falling off the low-calorie wagon. Don't let regression build momentum.

Adopting the Bad Attitudes of the Adults in One's Life

One activity I always do with my students is to have them think of an adult in their life—preferably a relative—who has a bad attitude. (I have yet to meet a kid who doesn't know someone like this.) Then I have them think about this person's negativity, complaining, whining, moaning, general rudeness, or hostility toward others.

Next, have students look at the circumstances of this person's life. Is this person basking in wealth? Does this person enjoy going to work each day? Is this person surrounded by warmth and smiles and buckets of friends? *Hmm*, I wonder if this person's inevitably poor circumstances are a coincidence, or is it that this person has such a strained existence with all the major areas of life because of their downer attitude?

Illuminating the direct link allows teens to clearly see the cause-and-effect relationship that exists between attitude and conditions.

Finally, I introduce the idea of role models and tell my students that the people who popped into their heads, whether they like it or not, are serving as behavioral role models to them right now. And their risk is that if they don't seek out different role models, or actively seek not to behave like the people they just thought about, they might very well turn into the exact type of person they don't want to become. (This is when the class becomes spookily quiet. For some kids, I'm even speaking about their dads or moms.) But what teens must realize is that adults with bad attitudes are to teenagers much like people with the flu, and unless kids actively seek out some sort of immunization, they are all too susceptible to catching these people's influenzas. Attitudes are both contagious and infectious.

Not Feeding Their Attitudes With Proper Nutrition

A positive attitude is very much like a plant that needs regular watering, and teens who do not make regular efforts to seek out a degree of positive mental nourishment for themselves have weakened defenses against finding themselves mired in negative, gloomy, sullen, or angry states. For whatever reason, the messy stuff in life doesn't seem to have a problem flourishing if it goes unattended, but the positive things in life require constant nourishment . . . or else they starve. Whether it's through listening to good music, reading quality books, keeping in solid physical shape, going to church, spending time with family members, or chillin' with close friends, teenagers need to actively feed their souls.

Doin' the Standards-Based Hip-Hop Thing

Teaching Teens to Be Tenacious

The best way I've found to get teenagers to become engaged in their own learning, remain focused on the same objective for long stretches of time, build academic skills, think critically, learn to work well with others, and benefit from having made mistakes all while having a whole lotta fun is by having them do things.

Yep, I have teens do things. All the time.

Some folks call it project-based learning. I call it simple common sense.

My teenagers don't want to be forced to sit in hard, plastic seats in library-style silence for hours on end, slog through thick, flavorless textbooks that weigh almost 5 pounds, or be made to memorize facts, data, stats, or key information that can easily be accessed on the Internet and further illuminated with a dozen links at the drop of a hat. Heck no. They want to get out of their chairs, burn off the energy roaring through their veins (created by the explosive combination of hormones and far too much sugar), and actually make something.

Or perform something.

Or build something, take pictures of something, invent something, or lay down a soundtrack of their favorite songs to something.

Teenagers want to *do* things. They want to gross one another out, they want to peek deep within, and they want to be rewarded for their desires to do this instead of being ostracized for wanting to do what seems as natural to them as jumping in the water seems to a landlocked duck.

Yep, teens want to be active, get their hands dirty, and explore learning

> **Teens want to be active, get their hands dirty, and explore learning through a multi-sensory approach that taps into other modalities of education beyond mere paper, pens, books, and bubble tests.**

through a multisensory approach that taps into other modalities of education beyond mere paper, pens, books, and bubble tests. Therefore, in my class, I do things.

And how do I do them? First and foremost, by looking to the content area standards of my curriculum.

That's right, before I do anything else, I turn my attention to the standards.

See, the standards are like the North Star by which I guide the journey of my class. When things get crazy, when cooperative learning groupings implode, when the information superhighway causes more collisions and confusion than it provides answers and expediency, when I look up into a sea of student chaos and say to myself, "What the heck is supposed to be going on in here again?" the standards are there for me as a compass, a navigation system onto which I gratefully grab hold. They are my unfailing guideposts as I leap off into having my students immerse themselves in projects that push the limits of their abilities as well as my own.

Plus, the higher-ups in my school system get all warm and fuzzy on the inside when they discover I'm incorporating their favorite buzzword, *standards-based learning*, into my curriculum.

Goodness, do they love to hear that.

Even when my kids are standing on one foot on the top ledge of a ladder in the hallway during lunch, trying to create a better sense of mise-en-scène for their video projects, it's always standards-based learning.

For example, in the language arts content area of the reading comprehension strand for grades 9/10 (the state of California combines the standards for these two grade levels into one strand instead of separate grade-level units), there is a section I am supposed to teach on informational materials and functional documents. The standard reads:

A bit of a mouthful, isn't it? More on that in a moment.

Now, when I first think of teaching the language arts, I think of teaching books and reading. And writing and grammar. And literary analysis and punctuation. And even Shakespeare. About a bazillion things leap to mind that, at first glance, seem to take precedence over teaching my students something as apparently mundane as functional documents. However, when I reflect more deeply on the matter, I realize that my students have a pretty good chance of getting through life if they don't ever intellectually digest something like how to dissect figurative language or explicate the difference between a simile and a metaphor. Yet, if they don't know how to properly read a set of directives, distinguish the real meaning behind the message in a household mailer, or comprehend and evaluate critical information that might be embedded inside the text of a set of instructions, they risk the chance of being duped by false advertising, missing out on a fantastic deal that could have saved them a lot of money, or entering into a contractual arrangement in which they agree to things they have no idea they are agreeing to.

The truth is, before Charles Dickens, Edgar Allan Poe, and Sylvia Plath, there are fast-food menus, auto repair coupons, and cellular telephone contracts to be understood, evaluated, tossed away, or clutched like the saviors to our financial lives that some of these types of documents can often be. Therefore, and with good reason, I make sure to tackle this content area of the standards in my class.

But of course, my goal is always to do it with pizzazz, something that will genuinely engage my students.

I begin any new project with a close analysis of the standard I've selected to teach and reread the fine print to make sure I genuinely understand what it is that the state is actually asking me to have my students do. And the irony is not lost on me that at the exact moment I am trying to figure out a means by which I can teach my students how to properly analyze and comprehend information from a functional document, I am being required to literally do so myself.

Personally, I find the content standards dry to read and difficult to understand. Often, I even ask myself after having just read some of the standards, "What the heck did that just say?"

And I know that I am not alone when I ask this question. Teachers all over seem to often scratch their heads when it comes to interpreting their state's academic learning objectives. To make things simple on myself, I've developed a system, a sort of *Standards Interpretation for Dummies*, which I use all the time.

To best break down and interpret the content standards, I begin with underlining the main verbs in the standard. Why the verbs? Because they tell me what I am supposed to have my students specifically do.

2.0 Reading Comprehension

Structural Features of Informational Materials: 2.1. <u>Analyze</u> the structure and format of functional documents, including the graphics and headers, and <u>explain</u> how authors use the features to achieve their purposes.

Okay, we are supposed to do two things. First we are supposed to *analyze* and second we are supposed to *explain*. Then I get a few 3-by-5 note cards, one for each verb, and I write on them:

ANALYZE	EXPLAIN

Next I go back and ask myself, "Analyze and explain what?" This is where I use the skills of paraphrasing, of putting things into my own words so that I know I clearly understand my directives.

ANALYZE	EXPLAIN
the structure and format of a funct doc, including graphics and headers	how the doc's author chose the feats to accomp his purp

Okay, now I get it. (Like I said, this is *Standards Breakdown for Dummies*, but if I am going to have a North Star for my classroom lesson, I had better make sure I fully understand the direction in which my star is pointing.)

Experience tells me, though, that tackling only one standard at a time for my classroom lessons is often not enough. This is because the content area standards quite frequently harmonize well when grouped in twos or threes, so often I'll scour about and see if something else matches up well with the standard I've chosen to teach.

And sure enough, one does.

I, of course, reread the standard, underline the main verbs, and go through the process of yet again making up my North Star note cards.

2.0 Reading Comprehension

Expository Critique: 2.7. <u>Critique</u> the logic of functional documents and <u>examine</u> the sequence of information and procedures in anticipation of possible reader misunderstandings.

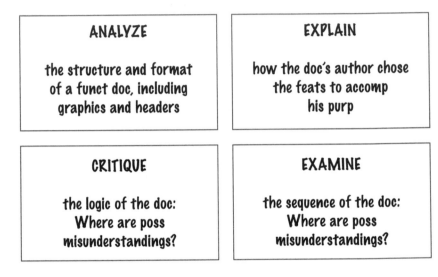

CRITIQUE

the logic of the doc:
Where are poss
misunderstandings?

EXAMINE

the sequence of the doc:
Where are poss
misunderstandings?

And then I lay all four of my cards in front of me so that I can see the forest for the trees.

ANALYZE

the structure and format
of a funct doc, including
graphics and headers

EXPLAIN

how the doc's author chose
the feats to accomp
his purp

CRITIQUE

the logic of the doc:
Where are poss
misunderstandings?

EXAMINE

the sequence of the doc:
Where are poss
misunderstandings?

Looking as I always am for a way to really hook my English classes at the start of anything I do, I decide to reach into my bag of razzle-dazzle tricks and break out the good ol'-fashioned peanut butter and jelly language arts lesson. Though teachers have known about this fun lesson for years, it's still a winner every time I reach for it. But of course, to add a little twist, I make sure to use organic peanut butter, which, when left unrefrigerated and unstirred, becomes this goopy, sludgy mess that never fails to draw even more heightened reactions from teenagers. Anything I can do to gross my students out is always a winner.

Basically, I assign all my students the task of writing down the directions for making a peanut butter and jelly sandwich. "Be thorough," I tell them. Then, once they've finished writing their instructions as to how to accomplish this task, I break out a jar of peanut butter, a jar of jelly, a loaf

of bread, plastic knives, paper plates, and napkins. Next I have students swap instructions and follow the *exact* directions for making a sandwich written by their partner. It's a great introductory activity for getting students to see the value of well-written functional documents because it forces students to recognize what happens when they don't use specific details in their writing. All I need are a few inexpensive supplies, and the smiles are never far behind. By forcing students to follow the directions literally, and I mean word for word, I end up with students having to do things such as stick their fingers inside the jar of peanut butter to spread the goop across the bread because the kid who wrote the instructions forgot to include tiny little details in his directions such as "use a knife."

Kids forget to mention opening the jar of jelly, sandwiches end up having the peanut butter and jam on the exterior side of the bread instead of the interior, and on and on. Fun, smiles, and a lesson well learned by the end of the day that writing functional documents is hard work and requires meticulous attention to detail set the stage for the next phase of my lesson plan.

Usually for homework on the day that precedes this lesson, I'll have my students bring in a bunch of menus the local restaurants are always leaving, much to most people's chagrin, on our front doors.

Why? Because we are going to analyze, critique, explain, and examine them. (Notice how my note card writing has given me the clarity to see my teaching objective.)

There is no right or wrong type of menu for this activity, and since I always give credit for all classroom assignments, this is a very easy way for every student in my class to earn points without doing any real intellectually heavy lifting at the start. (Sort of my own little trick to build up students' self-esteem. "This is so easy," they think. "Plus, I just had my fingers in a jar of jelly. This class is cool!")

Chinese food. Italian joints. Pizza parlors and sandwich shops—I see all sorts of menus. Of course I also take a wee bit of environmental satisfaction in knowing that instead of all these worthless menus going in the garbage, they'll get turned into educational tools for my classroom that will eventually be recycled so we can be green as well as well learned.

Next we look at the menus. Then we chat. Why is this menu effective? Why does this one stink? How come this menu makes me hungry and this one is pathetic and actually makes me not want to eat at the restaurant at all?

Answers fly, students break off into their own little bubbles of independent conversations, and menus get dissected from a host of interesting yet disparate angles.

After a full classroom dialogue, I pull out my own fast-food menu . . . and car wash coupon, real estate broker's mailer, and ad for breast enhancement surgery. (Trust me, this last one opens the door to fantastic dialogues about self-esteem, how women are objectified in society, the prejudice people hold against both girls with large chests and those with small ones; the chats are electric and weighty in many, many, ways.) All the pieces of paper I pull out, of course, are materials that I have lesson planned top to bottom before class even began so I can go through and teach all of the elements of functional documents I want to make sure my students comprehend.

Ultimately, by the time I am done, we, as a class, have analyzed, critiqued, explained, and examined the structure, format, graphics, headers, author choices, logic, sequence, purpose, and possible misunderstandings of functional documents in a way that engaged my students, related to their lives, was made accessible to all levels of learners in the class (from gifted and talented students to English language learners, they are all tuned in), and, most assuredly, brought some smiles to the faces of my kids.

Truthfully, probably very little of it even felt to them like learning.

However, the question then becomes, *How do I really know if my students have grasped the structure and function of informational documents?*

I mean, I think they have. My lesson seemed to go well, yet how can I be sure?

Through my own informal mode of assessment, my own observation, and dialogue with my students, I have definitely gained a strong sense that my kids have comprehended all that I had hoped to teach them. However, the fact of the matter is that *doing* is the most effective means by which I can get my students to really grasp the structure and format of functional documents. Doing means I'll have my kids go beyond reading, hearing, seeing, and talking about functional documents and elevate my lesson to where my students can and will create a functional document of their own.

And so we'll create our own hip-hop musical menus of the soundtracks to their lives. Kinda snazzy, huh? (See Figure 4–1.)

I make this functional document project music based because my students love music and music is often an area in life about which teenagers feel unbridled passion. Of course, I see a ton of hip-hop, but the truth is, this assignment can work just as well with any genre of music. Heck, I could step into a classroom in Nashville, Tennessee, and do the same lesson with country western music that I can do in inner-city Los Angeles with urban fare. Reggae, ska, punk, speed metal, or classical, the genre of music doesn't really matter. Nor does my content knowledge about the musical artists my kids prefer to listen to. After all, I'm as old as a

Figure 4–1 ❀ Musical Menu Project Assignment

Musical Menu Assignment Sheet

Assignment: Create a musical menu to the soundtrack of your life that views musical selections of your own choosing as if they were a well-harmonized meal to be deliciously digested.

Your restaurant will need to serve at least three well-selected appetizers, three well-selected first-course entrees, three well-selected second-course entrees, and three well-selected dessert items. (*Note:* You may add side dishes or a few extra goodies if you like.)

General description of the meal (feel free to make each item sound scrumptious, as restaurant menus often do):

- Appetizers introduce us to the tastes your musical menu will serve.
- First-course entrees provide solid substance to the meal but do not fill us up in entirety.
- Second-course entrees are the main portion of your musical meal, the critical, essential, can't-live-without elements to the musical menu.
- Desserts cap our dining experience. We could do without them, but often they add a nice sweetness to our entire experience.

Please make sure to cite the musical artist as well as the song title in each category.

The assignment needs to meet each of the following criteria:

- The menu conveys a clean, professional appearance.
- The menu offers three appetizers.
- The menu offers three first-course entrees.
- The menu offers three second-course entrees.
- The menu offers three desserts.
- The menu has an easy-to-read heading that tells us the name of your restaurant.
- The menu has an easy-to-read subheading that explains the theme of your restaurant.
- The menu has a mission statement that explains the ideological ambition of your restaurant.
- The menu has a border that includes a tasteful graphic design.
- The menu has an element of visual/pictorial art tastefully incorporated so as to add to, and not detract from, the menu.
- The menu uses three different font styles.
- The menu includes three different font sizes.
- All words on the document are properly spelled.
- The menu displays creativity.
- The assignment was completed in a timely manner.

Note: A grading rubric with clear expectations, point values, and specific parameters will be provided. Please consult it!

pterodactyl in the eyes of my students, and quite frankly, when it comes to today's music, I don't know the names of half the musicians or bands my students adore anyway.

But I don't need to. My kids will do all the heavy lifting on that side of teaching to the standards for me. I set the framework, I craft the assignment, but then I step back and let my students' own diverse, disparate, impossible-to-fit-into-one-similarly-sized-box interests step to the forefront of our work. No, the musical artists my students use for this assignment matter little, but what greatly matters is that my kids get to choose.

Choice makes teenagers feel empowered. Choice makes teenagers feel respected. Choice makes teenagers feel validated. By allowing teens to do schoolwork in an area that speaks directly to one of their most important outside-of-school interests (i.e., music), I get exceptional engagement and a high ambition to do high-quality work before I even pass out the details of the assignment. (See Figure 4–2 for the sample menu I present as a model for my class.) In order to avoid letting students too closely mimic my exemplar (i.e., pinching my ideas and creating a menu that is too close in content or ideas to the one I provide), I made my sample for a reading restaurant instead of a musical restaurant. The students still have a template, a solid example, but they are forced to craft their own internal logical structures to songs, artists, and the music they love without borrowing too heavily from my model of structure and function.

Ultimately, though, all of my success in this lesson hinges on the means by which I assess the students' work. As mentioned earlier, informal assessment (i.e., my own personal observation of the comprehension of the content standards) isn't adequate to prove solid proficiency of comprehension. Therefore, how I frame the assignment by means of directives, expectations, goals, and time frames, and how I evaluate my students both during the creation of their musical menus and upon the final completion and presentation of the task, is really where the rubber meets the road.

This is why I am such a *huge* fan of rubrics.

When it comes to having my students create projects, grading rubrics are the teacher tool that allows me to accomplish the many, many critical things I need to do in order to attain classroom success.

Rubrics allow me to set clear expectations for all students, provide firm guidelines as to what my assignments require, and make my evaluations more objective and fair to all kids across the board. Plus, rubrics make

Teecha's Restaurant
Where values are valued.

A Menu for Your Mind

Appetizers
(Life's Early Meals)

The Three Little Pigs, by the Grimm Brothers

The Boy Who Cried Wolf, by Aesop

The Ugly Duckling, by H. C. Andersen

First-Course Entrees
(Contemporary Fare)

Tears of a Tiger, by Sharon Draper

Monster, by Walter Dean Myers

Ender's Game, by Orson Scott Card

Second-Course Entrees
(Classic Fare)

King Lear, by William Shakespeare

Les Miserables, by Victor Hugo

Crime and Punishment, by Fyodor Dostoevsky

Dessert
(Life's Reflective Meals)

The King James Bible

The Upanishads

The New Testament

Our mission is to provide you with delicious mental meals
that will keep your brain fueled with the food your soul craves.

grading complicated projects much simpler and less time consuming. Yes, they take a lot of effort for me to create up front, but the time, clarity, and effectiveness I gain by using rubrics in my classroom more than make up for this investment in being well prepared to usher in classroom success, especially in a room full of reluctant readers and writers whose attention spans are tenuous in the first place.

> My classroom is not a field of learning to be littered with hidden land mines and potholes that are set like traps to catch my kids off guard and knock them down. I want all of my students to earn As for their efforts.

Rubrics also allow for transparency, both for my students and me. As the teacher, I must ask myself, "When I cook up all of my ambitious ideas, what do I want my students to know, prove, do, and show?" Without actually taking the time to literally write down the answers to these questions, instead of having clearly defined academic objectives in my brain, I often have something more akin to fuzzy concepts that I can sort of sense but can't really put my finger on. Writing things down forces me to define my ideas, crystallize my thoughts, and weigh whether or not they are sufficient, intelligent, convoluted, or harebrained. The first beneficiary of grading rubrics is, as I have discovered, always me, the teacher.

Once I've built my rubric and I know what it is that I want, I can then proceed to more clearly explain to my students all of the various components of the task I am assigning them. (See Figure 4–3.)

Without rubrics, I've learned, there are times when the gap between what I want and what my students think I want is so tremendous that even if they work hard and give a great effort, they ultimately miss the mark. And while I might want to blame my students for not really paying attention as I went over the mandates of the assignment, the truth is quite often that it was I who fell short in providing clarity for the demands of my assignment to my kids. Basically, I've come to the conclusion that there is no project for which I do not need a grading rubric in order to prevent miscommunication of the assignment to my students as well as misunderstandings about all of the various elements I require to see evidenced in the projects that they complete.

Figure 4–3 ❀ Musical Menu Project Rubric Straight Out of My Class

Musical Menu Project
Grading Rubric

_____ 20 points. . . . . The menu conveys a clean, professional appearance.

_____ 15 points. . . . . The menu offers three well-selected appetizers. *(5 points each)*

_____ 15 points. . . . . The menu offers three well-selected first-course entrees. *(5 points each)*

_____ 15 points. . . . . The menu offers three well-selected second-course entrees. *(5 points each)*

_____ 15 points. . . . . The menu offers three well-selected desserts. *(5 points each)*

_____ 10 points. . . . . The menu has an easy-to-read heading. *(Tells us the name of your restaurant)*

_____ 10 points. . . . . The menu has an easy-to-read subheading. *(Explains the theme of your restaurant)*

_____ 10 points. . . . . The menu has a mission statement. *(Explains the goal of your restaurant)*

_____ 10 points. . . . . The menu has a border. *(Includes a tasteful graphic design)*

_____ 10 points. . . . . The menu has visual art. (*Tastefully executed so as not to detract from the menu)*

_____ 15 points. . . . . The menu has three different font styles on display. *(5 points each)*

_____ 15 points. . . . . The menu has three different font sizes on display. *(5 points each)*

_____ 15 points. . . . . All words on document are properly spelled.

_____ 15 points. . . . . An effort to be uniquely creative is on display.

_____ 10 points. . . . . Assignment is completed in a timely manner.

_____ TOTAL SCORE out of 200 points

For example, when the language arts content standards of my state say I must have students analyze, explain, critique, and examine graphics and headers in a functional document, and my rubric explains to students that they need to create graphics and headers for their functional documents that can be analyzed, explained, critiqued, and examined at a level commensurate with my own high expectations for their work (I always ask more of my students than does the state), I can rest assured that my students know before they ever present their final projects to me that they'd better make sure they've created graphics and headers for their functional documents that will stand up in the face of my clear grading criteria.

Rubrics are checklists for my students.

Ultimately, I am also a great fan of rubrics because I truly want my students to succeed. My classroom is not a field of learning to be littered with hidden land mines and potholes that are set like traps to catch my kids off guard and knock them down. I want all of my students to earn As for their efforts, and rubrics, when it comes to project-based learning in my classroom, are the best tool I know to set clear expectations while giving my students a barometer by which they can measure their own efforts even before it comes time for me to grade them.

Heck, with a well-written rubric, most of my students can usually grade themselves.

You'll notice that I ask students to write mission statements for their restaurants. There are a few reasons for this. First, all successful businesses have a mission statement. Pepsi has a mission statement, Scholastic has a mission statement: even Lynwood High School has a mission statement. Second, writing a mission statement requires my students to think critically about the goals, values, strategies, and vision for their enterprise. I like to stretch my students' thought processes about whatever we are doing whenever I can. Finally, writing a mission statement for the restaurant also harmonizes well with another activity I have my students do every year: writing their own personal mission statements. It's a lesson I take straight from the pages of *The 7 Habits of Highly Effective Teens* (Covey 1998), a book we usually read in the early part of the school year, and since I always try to create a synergy between the ideas, novels, nonfiction, and projects I tackle, adding a mission statement to this restaurant menu assignment works well for me. In a way, it makes the functional document assignment more functional.

Additionally, I have a nebulous category, one that's most certainly subjective and difficult to quantify on a grading rubric: creativity. No, creativity is not measurable, yet I include this to make the bigger point to my teens that it's often the intangible factors of project-based learning—the nonquantifiable things—that frequently make the greatest difference to success.

Just as in life, the *je ne sais quoi*, that little something extra that can't be precisely defined and eludes description, is often the grand differentiator between mediocrity and greatness. I believe this is a very important lesson to teach.

Of course, most teachers don't create finely detailed lesson plans for every unit they teach (*ssshh*, don't tell the vice principal), yet I do find it useful to fill in the main areas of a unit lesson plan before I begin, for my own sense of clarity. Knowing all the angles of the assignment ahead of time helps a ton once teenage enthusiasm surrounding this project kicks into high gear. (See Figure 4–4.)

The standards may appear at first glance to be rigid, but the methodology of teaching to them is fantastically flexible. To wit, functional documents like menus also provide a nice way to think about the characters in our books from new and interesting perspectives.

Hey, why not have students create a restaurant menu based on the characters in *To Kill a Mockingbird* to prove their comprehension of literary characterization while creating functional documents at the same time?

(Yes, I do teach the classics once my students are ready for them. Why? Because as Carol Jago once said, "Our students deserve to read them." Great answer, huh?)

Atticus Finch would put dolphin-safe tuna on the menu because of his inner sense of morality and righteousness. Boo Radley would put Lynwood's lunchtime meatloaf on the menu because of his secretive nature (since we never really know what our school puts in the meatloaf anyway). And on and on. (See Figures 4–5 and 4–6 for a few examples of my students' work.)

Engaging books with engaging assignments anchored in standards-based teaching models: there is really no limit to the ways in which I can creatively embrace the interests of my students while remaining well rooted in the core classroom objectives. From James Joyce to Stephen King, an intelligent use of the standards allows me to keep it real with my teens while keeping it academically sound for my teaching objectives.

Now, do new ideas come to me all the time once I see my students in action? Of course they do. And do I always know what crazy direction I

Figure 4–4 🌑 Musical Menu Project Sample Lesson Plan

Subject: English Language Arts
Teacher: Alan Sitomer
Grade Level: Grade 10
Lesson Title: Musical Menus: A Functional Document Assignment

Academic Content Standards
2.0 Reading Comprehension
Structural Features of Informational Materials
2.1: Analyze the structure and format of functional documents, including the graphics and headers, and explain how authors use the features to achieve their purposes.

Expository Critique
2.7: Critique the logic of functional documents and examine the sequence of information and procedures in anticipation of possible reader misunderstandings.

Lesson Objective
The students will have analyzed, critiqued, explained, and examined the structure, format, graphics, headers, author choices, logic, sequence, purpose, and possible misunderstandings of functional documents in a way that was relative to their lives and was made accessible to all levels of learners in the class.

Essential Questions
1. How are all types of reading and writing similar to one another?
2. How can various types of reading and writing be different from one another?
3. What makes for a solid functional document?

Assessment
Entry-level assessment: A class conversation will explore, dissect, and take a close look at a host of functional documents in order to informally assess whether my students understand and comprehend the subject matter being presented to them.
Formative-level assessment: Students will create an outline of their musical menu by hand to be peer reviewed and then teacher reviewed as a stepping-stone to the creation of their own functional document.
Summative-level assessment: Students create their own functional document in accordance with the criteria for the assignment.

Method of Scoring
See rubric.

Figure 4–5   ❖   Student samples of projects I've received.

Figure 4–6 🌑 A menu a student did for *The Great Gatsby.*

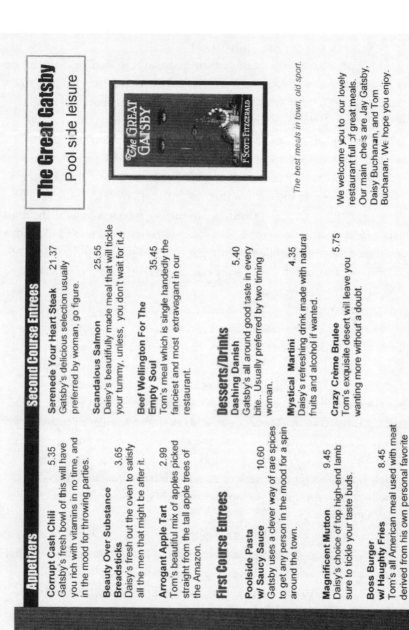

The Great Gatsby
Pool side leisure

The best meals in town, old sport.

We welcome you to our lovely restaurant full of great meals. Our main chefs are Jay Gatsby, Daisy Buchanan, and Tom Buchanan. We hope you enjoy.

Appetizers

Corrupt Cash Chili 5.35
Gatsby's fresh bowl of this will have you rich with vitamins in no time, and in the mood for throwing parties.

Beauty Over Substance Breadsticks 3.65
Daisy's fresh out the oven to satisfy all the men that might be after it.

Arrogant Apple Tart 2.99
Tom's beautiful mix of apples picked straight from the tall apple trees of the Amazon.

First Course Entrees

Poolside Pasta w/ Saucy Sauce 10.60
Gatsby uses a clever way of rare spices to get any person in the mood for a spin around the town.

Magnificent Mutton 9.45
Daisy's choice of top high-end lamb sure to tickle your taste buds.

Boss Burger w/ Haughty Fries 8.45
Tom's all American meal used with meat derived from his own personal favorite selection.

Second Course Entrees

Serenede Your Heart Steak 21.37
Gatsby's delicious selection usually preferred by woman, go figure.

Scandalous Salmon 25.55
Daisy's beautifully made meal that will tickle your tummy, unless, you don't wait for it.4

Beef Wellington For The Empty Soul 35.45
Tom's meal which is single handedly the fanciest and most extravagant in our restaurant.

Desserts/Drinks

Dashing Danish 5.40
Gatsby's all around good taste in every bite... Usually preferred by two timing woman.

Mystical Martini 4.35
Daisy's refreshing drink made with natural fruits and alcohol if wanted.

Crazy Crème Brulee 5.75
Tom's exquisite desert will leave you wanting more without a doubt.

am going to impulsively want to go at 10:30 at night when I have a flash of insight as to the next cool thing I think I can do? Of course not. And I feel that's a good thing. As the old saying goes, "Some educators teach for thirty years; others teach one year thirty times."

I want my class to be vibrant, attuned, sensitive to feedback, and adaptable to the needs of my kids as I understand them over the course of the year. Knowing exactly what I am going to teach in the month of April when it's only October means that I'm not really teaching the kids—I'm teaching the program, and the kids must adapt and conform in order to achieve classroom success when really, the most flexible person in the room needs to be me, the educator. After all, there are usually 35 of them and only one of me, and each of them is different. With so many various needs, aptitudes, likes, and dislikes, I'm the one who has to wear the most hats and be the most malleable. I've got to be tough on the soft kids and soft on the hard ones while remaining open enough to shift directions on a dime yet firm enough to drive my classroom on through a snowstorm of interruptions and adversity.

Teaching from the perspective such as the one I have described here allows me to do all of these things. I can witness my students' strengths, focus on their deficiencies, and tailor new lessons as I go, based on the feedback I see from their daily work. I get to use cooperative groupings, peer review, graphic organizers, into-through-beyond methodology, growth model evaluations, newspaper articles ripped from the day's headlines, poems written 500 years ago, and, as you've seen, even supermarket groceries. (Which I am still hoping the state picks up the bill for one of these days. Don't they see how critical peanut butter is to my English class?) Now, does it take a heck of a lot of effort? Of course it does. But what in this world that proves to be worthwhile doesn't take a lot of effort to accomplish?

Now, do I run into problems along the way? Sure. But between my students and me and the myriad of resources I have on my campus—that is, my peers on the staff and the other students in the hall—I can usually find the answers to the things that vex me as I trek along this road-not-taken path. The only thing I really have to remember at all times is to be tenacious.

Be tenacious!

Be tenacious in terms of getting your classroom discipline in order. Be tenacious in terms of getting the physical sense of your room to a place where it is comfortable for you and your students to be productive. Be tenacious when it comes to figuring out your essential questions, how best to synchronize disparate standards, create a grading rubric, conceptualize a unit you've never taught before, or crack the riddle as to how to get people off your back for not towing the line when it comes to their peddling ineffective, boring curriculum.

If you are going to be successful in the modern-day classroom, you must be tenacious.

And then teach this skill to your teens.

Teach Teens to Be Tenacious

When you work with teens for long enough, you realize that many of your own biggest insights into your students don't come during instructional time but rather on the edges, as you interact with them during passing periods, after school, when they are eating lunch in your room, and so on. During class, they often show you masks of who they want to project (i.e., the student that you see through the lens of being a teacher). But during "human" time, they show you much more of who they really are, intentionally or not.

And goodness—what I got to see the week of the local radio contest!

A few years ago, the number one local hip-hop station was holding a competition to see which high school could win an on-campus Friday performance by the latest, greatest, hip-hop musical group. It set my school on fire. The contest was announced on a Friday morning before classes began, and by lunchtime, it seemed like the entire student body had organized itself into an army of callers and e-mailers. (The most calls and e-mails within a week would win.)

At first, it was amusing. The students were jumping out of their skin with excitement. (And really, is there a higher level of human energy capable of being exerted than that of a teenage girl in pursuit of her favorite musician? Now multiply that by a few thousand, mix in the fact that it was a Friday, and you can imagine the buzz zapping through campus.)

I went home that weekend and completely forgot about the radio contest. But my students certainly didn't. On Monday I was met before class at 6:55 A.M. by three girls, Sharice and her two lieutenants.

"Mr. Alan," she asked, "can the whole class have the day off today?"

First, I was shocked to see Sharice in my room so early because she was the kind of student who usually rolled in 8 seconds before the tardy bell (and sometimes 15 minutes after). What was she doing here half an hour early? And with such an unreasonable request?

"Uhm, no," I answered.

"But we in the top five, Mr. Alan," Sharice exclaimed, bursting with excitement. "We in the top five!"

It turns out that Lynwood students had spent the entire weekend barraging the radio station with calls and e-mails and were now in the top five vying for the hip-hop performance the station would be sponsoring at a local high school at the end of the following week. Now, while this might not seem remarkable, Los Angeles is a *huge* city, and when one of the top musical groups in the country is coming to town for a special show, the competition to win is fierce. Sharice wanted to cancel class so that all the students could break out their cellies and spend the entire day calling up the radio station to score more points.

"Nice idea," I said. "But no."

Sharice pouted for a moment, then left to go talk strategy with a team of other students before class began. Though we are a gigantic high school (more than 4,000 students some years), we are not the biggest high school in the city and the schools ahead of us in the radio station voting were even larger than we were. So basically, we were underdogs.

However, on Tuesday Lynwood had somehow clawed its way into the top three. By Thursday, we had moved up to number two. Frenzy filled the halls. It was as if Beatlemania had hit, and as a teacher, I could not help but marvel at Sharice. Here was a student with a 1.43 GPA who frequently gave minimal effort when it came to doing any of her school work, yet, with the chance to win a campus hip-hop performance, she was diligent, demanding, organized, focused, tireless, and frighteningly determined. Plus, as the week went on, her efforts grew stronger, like a marathon runner who gains strength at the twenty-fourth mile marker.

On Friday morning it was announced that Lynwood had won. We'd be getting a free concert. Sharice was ecstatic.

At the show the students went crazy. I'd never seen Sharice so happy. Then, the following Monday, when my students got back to class, I made it a point to tell them about how much I loved bulldogs. Fighters. About how people who battled through obstacles, overcame hurdles, and clawed their way toward achieving goals in spite of apparently huge hurdles were people who were going to be okay in this world, regardless of what was thrown at them. And Lynwood students had just defied the odds and won a concert for themselves in a way that showed grit, effort, and fantastic determination.

Being the dorky teacher that I am, you can see how I sought to use the radio event to make a bigger point about the importance of tenacity. I even wrote the word T-E-N-A-C-I-T-Y on the board that day and centered my class lesson around the idea that hey, this is how life works. Tenacity leads to triumph.

Additionally, seeking the teachable moment with Sharice, I made sure to keep her after class and specifically spell out for her how, if she pursued her education with the same zest that she pursued winning this local radio station contest, she could escape the poverty, violence, and depravity of her current environment in Lynwood. (At the time, Sharice was living with her grandmother while her mother served time in jail.)

My conversation with Sharice went in one ear and right out the other. Sadly, her efforts never rose above that of a kid earning a report card full of Ds.

Aargh! It's the kind of thing that makes you want to pull out your hair from the roots.

On the other hand, another year I had a student named Raphael. Instead of telling you his tale, I'll let you (with Rafi's permission) read his college essay application. (See Figure 4–7.)

While I have had students earn acceptance to Stanford, the University of California (UC) at Berkeley, the University of Southern California (USC), and the University of California at Los Angeles (UCLA) among other schools, Rafi was the first student I ever had to be admitted to the Massachusetts Institute of Technology (MIT). (See Figure 4–8.)

Now, I don't care where you teach; when one of your kids gets accepted to MIT, you feel like clicking your heels. However, while Rafi was most assuredly one of the brightest kids I've ever had in class, brains were not the reason he was off to Massachusetts. Tenacity was. Fortitude was. Work ethic was. (And by that I mean his, not mine. I don't claim to be the reason

Figure 4–7   Rafi's College Essay

Prompt for Essay B: Describe the world you come from, for example, your family, clubs, school, community, city, or town. How has that world shaped your dreams and aspirations?

Ever since I can remember, my sister Patty has been in jail for either drug use, theft or gang-banging. I've started off some high school courses sitting on the floor for two weeks because of overcrowded classrooms. I walk home every day down streets filled with graffiti, drug dealers and prostitutes. How has this world shaped my aspirations? By instilling in me the relentless desire to pursue a college degree. If there is one thing I know to be true from firsthand experience it's that the only way to change things for the better in my community will be from the inside out. And first it starts with me.

    I have done much to thrive in spite of the obstacles persistent in my environment. I cannot stop the tagging, the prostitution, or the gangs. I cannot stop my peers from getting pregnant or dropping out. But what I can do is get the best education I can possibly obtain. Often I had to look elsewhere to enrich my opportunities. I've enrolled in college classes while still in high school, asked teachers one-to-one about subject material beyond the scope of the class, and read extensively on my own about topics of great interest to me. I also joined clubs to expand my educational opportunities. Most importantly though, through ambition, determination, and resilience, I have turned what could have been a world of depravity and ignorance into a landscape of opportunity.

    The traits I developed in pursuing a better education have also proven beneficial to other endeavors, whether it involved academic competitions, athletics, or simply learning new skills. When our novice trebuchet team was ridiculed and told we had no chance, we forged on and ended up placing 3rd in regional competition despite numerous obstacles. When my very own teachers told me how hard the AP tests were and claimed I'd be lucky if I got a 3 on even one of them, I studied and studied and ended up passing multiple exams with 4s and 5s. I joined track even though I was hardly what one would call athletic and I trained for hours a day until I was finally able to vault. When presented with the opportunity to go to Washington D.C. to attend the 2004 presidential inauguration, I did not give up when I learned of the cost. Instead I sold Rice Krispies bars until I finally raised the whopping $800. Essentially I have learned to take initiative.

    No matter where I go, I am determined to be successful. I am going to find a way to make it beyond the inner city. I want to be pushed to my limits. Ultimately, I have learned that I am the person who will solely determine my fate and I am confident I have what it takes to succeed at the next level and beyond.

Figure 4–8  Rafi's MIT Acceptance Letter

Office of Admissions

MIT

Massachusetts Institute of Technology
77 Massachusetts Avenue, Building 3–108
Cambridge, Massachusetts 02139–4307

Phone 617-253-3400
Fax   617-258-8304
admissions.mit.edu

December 14, 2007

Mr. Raphael

Lynwood, CA 90262

Dear Raphael,

On behalf of the Admissions Committee, it is my pleasure to offer you admission to the MIT Class of 2012. You stood out as one of the most talented and promising students in one of the most competitive applicant pools in the history of the Institute. Your commitment to personal excellence and principled goals has convinced us that you will both contribute to our diverse community and thrive within our academic environment. We think that you and MIT are a great match.

You have until May 1, 2008 to let us know if you'll call MIT home for the next four years. Until then, we look forward to building our relationship with you and helping you to get to know us better. Over the next several months, we'll be in touch via phone, email, and web.

Because there's no better way to get a taste of life at MIT than to spend some time here, I hope very much that you will attend our Campus Preview Weekend (CPW) for admitted freshmen, held on campus from April 10-13, 2008. You'll attend classes, share meals and conversations with current students, and experience all the ways in which people spend their time and live their passions at MIT. (And most importantly, you'll get to meet your future classmates!) Look for a new CPW portlet in your MyMIT account in January, which will contain schedule and registration information.

And now for the requisite fine print – I must remind you that this offer of admission is contingent upon your completing the school year with flying colors. (Because you've been admitted early, there will be many temptations throughout the rest of the year to keep you from your schoolwork. Please don't let that happen!)

I hope you'll agree with us that MIT is the perfect place to prepare for your future. As a member of our community, you'll join builders, scholars, entrepreneurs, and humanitarians. Together, you will make all the difference in a world that desperately needs you.

Many congratulations, best wishes for a wonderful holiday season, and welcome to MIT! (Now stop reading this and go celebrate. :-)

Sincerely,

Interim Director of Admissions

my students get into these outstanding colleges. However, I'd be lying if I did not admit my hope that my efforts did, in some small way, contribute to their journeys.)

Like most teachers, I've had plenty of kids with brains and talent sitting in the chairs of my room. However, the fallacy we in the school systems promote to far too many kids is that it's the God-given gray matter inside their heads that will be the primary factor determining whether or not they will one day attain success.

It's simply not true.

Heart, soul, guts . . . these are the vital ingredients. And without these, kids are cooked. As one of my favorite presidential quotes says:

> *Nothing in this world can take the place of persistence. Talent will not; nothing is more common than unsuccessful men with talent. Genius will not; unrewarded genius is almost a proverb. Education will not; the world is full of educated derelicts. Persistence and determination alone are omnipotent. The slogan "Press On" has solved and always will solve the problems of the human race.*

> —Calvin Coolidge, thirtieth president of
> the United States (1872–1933)

Teach teens to be tenacious. As my beloved grandfather repeated many, many times to me over the course of my adult life, "Chop wood; chips fall."

Tips for Teaching Tenacity

Know That Tenacity Takes Time

As an English teacher, I was trained to teach skills such as how to properly use a colon in a sentence by assigning a writing task and then breaking out my red pen and pointing out all the errors of my kids' work right after they had made their first, best attempt to grasp this element of written grammar. And of course their papers would be littered with mistakes and I would return the essays with so much red on them it looked as though I'd cut myself shaving while grading them. Then one day it dawned on me that hey, learning how to use a colon properly in a sentence takes time. A lot of time. So instead of pointing out where they messed up, I started pointing out where they had succeeded, no matter how small and incremental their growth. (Eventually, I halted the scribbling of any negative comments whatsoever on their papers for pretty much the first two months of school. More on that in Chapter 6).

Amazingly enough, they started to grow as writers and I started to get more and more properly "colonized" papers. Additionally, I also started getting more and more questions on how to help guide their efforts as my students were in the middle of the writing process so that they could properly punctuate their work. Why? Because it takes time to learn skills (in both English class and life) and if the very first time you slip up someone is right there with a red pen to point it out, it makes you want to crawl in a hole and not give any more effort again.

Same goes for skills like learning to be tenacious. Kids are gonna slack at times. Being the voice of inspiration during the times they are forging ahead is much more effective than being the voice of belittlement when they lag behind. Remember, with teens, it's a marathon, not a sprint, and over the long haul they respond best to people who believe in them, even when they don't fully believe in themselves. View growth on a spectrum and not in isolated snapshots (which aren't really ever fair to anyone) and you'll be sure to see improvement.

Seek to Tap the Talent and Strengths in Teens That Already Exists

A famous story is told about Michelangelo. Upon the completion of his masterpiece sculpture *David*, one of his apprentices looked up and said, mesmerized by the statue's beauty, "Sir, you have created a work of absolute genius."

"No," Michelangelo replied thoughtfully. "The absolute genius was always there. All I did was release it from inside the marble."

In a lot of ways I feel the same way about working with teens. Truly, we spend so much of our time focused on teaching teenagers new skills that they do not yet possess that we forget to tap and develop the immense number of skills they already do possess. Teens are tenacious. Teens are determined. Teens are focused and persistent and goal oriented. (And if you don't think so, it's probably because they are not focused on the things that you want them to be focused upon, so who's the problem really with?) Just don't forget to tap the abilities that already exist inside of teens and then expand upon them. Bodybuilders don't acquire new biceps; they vigorously exercise the ones they already have until each muscle ripples.

Watch for the Three Enemies of Tenacity

Procrastination

If there is one element that almost universally sabotages teenagers of all kinds, it's procrastination. Every time I assign a reflective paper in which I ask my students to identify their own Achilles' heel (this ties to a little Greek mythology I do), the lion's share of my kids tell me that it's that they procrastinate *way* too much.

Procrastination is a monster. It's to be feared, identified, and expediently rooted out when it rears its ugly head because the only things it ever causes in teenagers are lesser performances, lost opportunities, frustration, stress, lowered self-esteem, and, of course, boatloads of wasted time.

Now of course, some teens will claim they work better under the pressure of waiting until the last minute.

Pelican poop. I don't buy it.

Be vigilant in respecting Newton's first law, which says that an object at rest tends to stay at rest and an object in motion tends to stay in motion. Once teens are striving toward a goal, keep a vigilant eye out for the pit of quicksand that is procrastination.

Digital Burnout

When I was a teen, I simply did not have 24/7 access to nonstop information, entertainment, and communication, but today's kids can plug in and push the pedal to the digital metal 'til their eyes pop out of their heads. Naturally, at some point kids get fatigued. Therefore, if you are going to expect teens to give out a ton of energy as far as pursuing goals tenaciously, you are going to have to make sure that they replenish themselves at some point, too, and unplug. Otherwise, kids fade, weariness sets in, and teenagers lose interest in their work.

Watch out for digital burnout. It subtly, yet nefariously, saps a teenager's will to keep on keepin' on.

A Diminishment of Encouragement

It's easy to go on a diet. Matter of fact, I know people that go on 15 to 20 of them every year. The hard part is staying on a diet when jelly doughnuts are singing love songs to you at dinner. This is why it's so important for teens to remain nourished by voices of encouragement, hope, and inspiration. Teenagers will begin things with every zesty intention in the world of seeing them through, but, as I tell my students every year, it's easy to be excited and fired up to earn an A in English the first week of class. The hard part is when I'm requiring them to bang out thoughtful critical insights on Tuesday nights in the middle of March when there isn't a lick of respite from more and more essays from me in sight for a heck of a long time.

Remember, the best way to make sure teens have the proper gas in their tanks to forge on during the tough days of remaining committed is to constantly feed their inspiration. As soon as kids start to feel discouraged, demoralized, disheartened, or dejected, all sorts of doors to disengagement begin to pry open. Be generous with your encouragement and perpetually inspire them: "Eyes on the prize, bay-bee! Remember what it's all about!"

5

The Secret Sauce
Teaching Teens That Education Pays

I smile at school. I smile on day 1, I smile on day 180, and any day I don't smile in between is a day I am probably not as effective as an educator as I could be.

I smile all the time. I believe in its power.

But I also believe in discipline because the fact of the matter is, if teachers don't have classroom management, they don't have anything. It's an inarguable truth. If you don't have classroom management, you simply can't teach.

So, what's the secret to classroom management? In my room, it's fizzy orange soda.

That's right, fizzy orange soda pop, the kind that has so much sugar and other chemicals in it that if you wanted to clean the rust off a garden tool, you'd simply soak your equipment in a gallon of it overnight and let the magic bubbles of modern soft drinks take their course.

Fizzy orange soda is my secret to classroom management because I let kids drink it in class if they want. Even if it's 6:55 A.M.

I let them chew gum, too. Or sip water if they prefer. Even caramel Frappuccinos don't bother me. (Of course I try to steer them in the direction of healthy choices, but hey, these are teens; I'm not a miracle worker!) When I do this, I feel my message to teenagers is clear: I trust you can still pay attention to the lesson, I know you're not an infant whose behavior needs to be micromanaged, and I expect that by granting you the latitude to act like an adult who can handle the challenge of enjoying a beverage while working at a desk, you will behave like an adult and take care of all the things that you are being asked to do in my room.

I find that if I treat teens like responsible people, they act like responsible people. In a way, it's a self-fulfilling prophesy. My students clean up their own messes, don't stick gum under their desks when they are done chewing it but rather get up and go throw it away, and make an effort to keep our classroom—not my classroom, *our* classroom—clean (as opposed to viewing it as a room in which they are not vested, which they then feel can be trashed without remorse). No, students can't roll on in with a McDonald's pancake breakfast and start spreading syrup all over the place while I prepare to teach how to properly punctuate an appositive phrase—it's just too much of a disruption—but I have yet to see any evidence that says that sucking on a lollipop during English class detracts from a student's ability to comprehend the tenets of identifying figurative language.

Orange juice is cool, Egg McMuffins are not, and recycling bins—with posters that commend the environmental intelligence we demonstrate when we recycle cans, bottles, and paper—help us stay green and clean.

Basically, I believe that in the smallest of ways, my students are always paying attention to how I treat them and if they feel that I am being condescending, hypocritical, unfair, or oppressive, they will take umbrage, a problem that can interfere with my ability to reach them. Besides, I'm drinking water or tea all day long myself, and fair is fair, right?

Ultimately, my belief is that people work best when they are comfortable, their physical needs are met, and they feel emotionally safe and well respected. I know I do. This line of thinking is the guiding force behind my bathroom pass policy.

I leave my bathroom pass next to the front door, and if students feel they need to use the restroom, they can get up, take the pass, and excuse themselves. No need to ask my permission. No need to double-check with me about it being okay to go. It's an open, unqualified invitation.

Plus, there is nothing that drives me loonier than being in the middle of a class discussion, asking a riveting question about a deep philosophical conundrum, you know, the kind of question that really is at the height of Bloom's, Socrates', Gardner's, and Maslow's apexes of learning, and having a student shoot a hand up and ask . . .

"Can I use the bathroom?"

Nothing deflates me more.

The bathroom pass is always right by the front door, and I tell my students on day 1, "You have about five minutes to take the pass, use the restroom, and return to class. Also, please put the bathroom pass back where it belongs, because there are usually more than thirty other people in the room and someone else might be waiting for your return to use the restroom, too. One pass at a time is all I provide."

Now, do I care if they get a drink of water, blow their nose, or just take a minute to get a breath of fresh air? Not really. Of course all teachers must ultimately decide their own policies, but for me, when a student asks for a bathroom pass, especially a female student, am I ever really going to say no to the question anyway? Of course not.

However, if a kid is gone for an excessive amount of time, that student never gets to go to the bathroom again. Period. It's not fair to me, it's not fair to the other students, and it's not fair to the environment in which we are all trying to work, an environment of mutual respect and responsibility. "You wanna go kick it with your homies for half an hour during English class? Okay, fine. But you're gonna have to cross your legs for the rest of the darn school year if you mess with me on this," I tell them at the start of the year.

Warnings like this, empty as they probably are, since of course I'll let the kids go to the bathroom should they need to (hey, you have to be a good bluffer to run a tight educational ship), pretty much get me through the year.

Now, yes, I admit, the atmosphere in my room is casual. And the procedures seem lax. And sometimes when people enter my classroom, I know it looks more like a teenage mosh pit than it does a standards-based, academically rigorous institution of fundamentally sound learning. But a causal atmosphere does not mean there is no structure. A structureless class would never work. Matter of fact, it'd be an outright catastrophe.

Ultimately, my entire philosophy as to how I approach classroom management can be boiled down to my simple belief that before the students in my room are students, they are people. It's that basic. And since unfortunately the process of schooling to the wi-fi, hip-hop teenagers of today far too often feels like nothing more than a trip through an educational factory, as if they were some kind of widget to be molded in accordance with a certain set of guidelines, I find one of my greatest allies in the quest to educate my kids is a simple respect for their fundamental personhood.

This is also why I don't have seating assignments or use a seating chart in my class. The way I figure it, if I need a seating chart to know everyone's name (and there are a lot of names, about 175 new ones each year . . . plus all the kids from the prior years and then the staff of about 150—managing 200 to 300 names on any given day is commonplace), then how am I ever going to learn more deeply about them as individual people, about their strengths and weaknesses, likes and dislikes, aptitudes and deficiencies and personalities?

Yep, in my class, sit wherever the heck you'd like. And if I have to move a student because the choice of seats provides too much socialization and not enough education, then I tell the kid, "Look, I'll move you only twice. Once is across the room. The second time is out the door."

Not with a referral or anything like that, mind you. In all the years I've been teaching at Lynwood, I can recall writing only one referral, and part of the reason for that was simply to see what would come of it if I looked to folks outside my class to handle my in-class behavior matters.

Let's just say I was spectacularly underwhelmed and haven't written another referral since. Teachers with a few years under their belts don't count on the front offices for classroom management assistance unless matters have escalated to a very high level. Novice educators show up at school thinking they have a team of administrators behind them to handle the unruly, test-you-to-your-limits teens and are shocked to find out that to be a teacher nowadays in a school like mine means you're pretty much on your own as far as behavior, language, and interactions are concerned unless there are felonies being perpetrated in your classroom. (Okay, that's a tongue-in-cheek comment, but you get the point.)

Therefore, in my classroom, I keep the policy simple. "Yo, there's the door." If students don't want to be there, they can feel free to leave. And if they can't behave in a manner that works for the class as a whole, *bye-bye*. No, there will be no visits to the dean, no trips to the principal's office, no excommunication to the Dungeon of Schoolhouse Discipline where poorly behaved children are sent to be reprimanded, shamed, scolded, or reformed. None of it. I just point to the door and tell my students, "Any time you want to leave, go ahead, because at the end of the day, I'm not going to be the one that will get you.

"Karma will."

See, I let my students know the very first week of school that I'm not there to slam them with classroom work they find grueling and meaningless. Nor am I there to be their baby-sitter, jailer, or oppressor. I view my role as being there to serve them; I work for them, they are my customers, and everything that we do in my class is, in my opinion, for their benefit. My goal is to empower them with valuable, tangible, important skills that they are going to need one day, and as I often tell my students, if they do not see how the things we are doing in class will one day be of significance to them, they should feel free to ask me. Really, they can just raise their hands and ask me with the full expectation that I will be able to provide them with a legitimate, no-BS answer as to why what I am asking them to do, as students, is meaningful. I'm a great fan of transparency. I believe students should always know why we are doing what we are doing, whether it's learning how to become more critical thinkers, more skilled writers, or more highly competent readers.

> Unfortunately, to the wi-fi, hip-hop teenagers of today far too often the process of school feels like nothing more than a trip through an educational factory, as if they were widgets to be molded in accordance with a certain set of guidelines.

"We're doing this because I said so" strikes me as a hollow, hurtful, dismissive, and condescending response when students ask, "Yo, why are we doin' this?" I know it's an answer that would certainly never work for me if the tables were turned. Truly, I believe that students are entitled to know why we're studying something, why I feel it's important to study, and how it will help serve them later on in their lives.

And if I don't have that answer, the real question then becomes *Why the heck am I teaching this?*

As I've learned, teens often view their parents and teachers as if they are the enemy. The obstacle. The barrier to the life they hope to lead. "But me," I tell my kids, "I view my job as that of your ally, and in this world, I think you're going to discover that the more of them you have, the better off you are going to be."

To many of my students, I've discovered, this is an entirely new and unique lens through which they can view a classroom teacher, a perspective that often helps me to disarm and reroute the behavior of kids with a particularly notorious past of acting out in the classroom.

"And if you don't want to be here, feel free to leave," I reiterate, "because, at the very least, I certainly can't allow you to disrupt the education of the people in this room who do want to be here. There's the door. Anyone who wants can just go."

I've never had a kid leave yet. I have, however, had to boot a few out. But usually they return of their own volition the next day with a much better attitude about matters. Look, kids are going to test you no matter who you are, so having a firm line in the sand is an absolute must and, yes, my rules may be few, but they absolutely get enforced. A teacher who barks but does not bite will eventually get whacked by the students.

Remember, Teens Are Choosing to Be There

Of course, running hand in hand with this approach to classroom management is my underlying knowledge that all of the kids in my room do want to be there. And do want an education. And think of themselves as smart, capable, intelligent, and deserving. I know this because the ones that don't want to come to school don't come. They just don't show up. The fact is, it's just far too easy to drop out of school in modern-day America.

In seventh grade, 12-year-old kids who are truant will be chased and pursued and punished for ditching lots and lots of class.

In eighth grade, 13-year-old kids who are truant will be chased and pursued and punished for ditching lots and lots of class.

By ninth grade, 14-year-old kids who are truant will be somewhat chased and somewhat pursued and kind of punished for ditching lots and lots of class.

In tenth grade, 15-year-old kids who are truant might be slightly chased, halfheartedly pursued, and barely punished for ditching lots and lots of class.

By the second half of tenth grade, they don't even chase a 15-year-old kid anymore because the stack of eighth-grade truants is so big and because the overworked counselors and truant officers know it's better to spend their energies on the younger kids who still have a chance of being reached. Look, when an overtaxed system meets cynical, overworked, underresourced employees, something's gotta give.

And the students all know this.

By eleventh grade, the age of 16, the school system legally allows teens to drop out.

All this means that despite the fronts my kids put up, if deep down they really didn't want an education, didn't believe in its value, weren't hoping for someone to break through and genuinely reach them, they wouldn't even be in my classroom at that moment. Knowing this, of course, helps me a great deal when it comes to classroom management because it shows me that hey, me and my teens, we're on the same side.

Of course, every teacher develops an individual style of classroom management, and trying to replicate mine could end up as a complete and total disaster for someone else. My approach may sound cheeky, it may sound lackadaisical, or it may sound just flat-out stupid. But I know there are times when I drive my kids as hard as any championship swim coach during a predawn workout, and my students rise to the challenge, which means to me that, when all is said and done, my approach to classroom management works.

At least for me it does, and at the end of the day, when it comes to classroom management, that's all that really matters.

In sports it is sometimes said that the best defense is a good offense. Well, when it comes to classroom management, sometimes the best behavior management tool available is a rich, engaging curriculum. Truly, I don't think I can even separate a well-managed classroom and an engaging curriculum. Veteran teacher Susan Ohanian (1982) once wrote that boredom and mischief could be kept at arm's length with school projects that engaged a student's body, mind, and heart. Essentially, that's what I seek to do; I work to find out what my kids are passionate about and then create curriculum that hooks them right from the start.

But, then again, there was the time that my laid-back management style completely blew up in my face.

Making It Happen

The great part about teaching classic literature is that it offers so many prisms through which a student can gain access to the deep themes and questions of life that are relevant and very much alive in the hearts and minds of teenagers today. *The Odyssey* allows me to enter into thoughtful conversations about temptation, about the difference between wants and needs, and about how, when desires morph into lusts, they are often harbingers of our own downfall. *The Strange Case of Dr. Jekyll and Mr.*

Hyde allows my students to explore the duality that exists in all people, the battle between good and evil that often lurks, yet rages, within us all. *Romeo and Juliet* allows my students to explore deep thinking about love and teenage romance, about unreasonable parental expectations and family loyalty, some of the grandest and most salient themes for all teenagers at their current stage of life. And *Animal Farm* allows me to jump into a deep analysis of propaganda, of its impact on how we behave, and of how manipulation of public messaging can often be one of the most effective, yet nefarious, tools there is to accomplish a person's—or in this case a group of pigs'—aims. When my students read *Animal Farm*, we cover oppression, impressions, truth, lies, and image versus reality.

And then we relate it all to modern media through a final, culminating project on propaganda in which I have my students create their own TV commercials. It's a project they adore.

A few reasons leap to mind as to why I am such a tremendous fan of this project. First off, the engagement is always spectacularly high. Instead of simply reading about the various techniques of propaganda in a boring textbook, we bring the techniques to life through technology (something my students always love to use). Additionally, my students have been inundated their entire lives with propaganda, and by creating a commercial for themselves, they often get to analyze the tools of manipulation companies use to try to convince them to buy their products. Any time we really break down a TV commercial and dissect its elements, it never fails to amaze everyone how stupid these companies feel their audience is. After all, if not, why would they speak to all of us in such obviously condescending and manipulative ways?

As a result of this unit, my students also become better informed about how to identify veracity in information, an essential skill since they, more so than any generation before them, are being bombarded with propaganda at an earlier age than ever. By the time we show a few commercials and break them down, my students see the medium of advertising in a whole new, critical light.

Plus, it's a project that helps me make sure my kids do not become victims of the Digital Divide.

In this world, there are basically two kinds of students: those who know how to use technology well and those who don't. It's that simple. And for the kids who don't have the technological skills they'll need to be successful in an ever-more-globalized and technologically driven society, trouble lies ahead. Essentially, it's the Haves versus the Have-Nots. In my Title I school, already hampered by limited resources in far too many ways, I'm driven to make sure my students are as intellectually, academically, and technologically competitive as they can be.

And I'm not talking about being able to compete with other kids at Lynwood High School; I want to make sure my kids can compete with the students at Beverly Hills High School, a school that is less than 15 miles—yet a world away—from our campus.

So basically, with limited resources, limited abilities, and limited time to accomplish everything I hope to, the rule for pulling off projects like my propaganda video commercial becomes "Make it happen."

> **In this world, there are basically two kinds of students: those who know how to use technology well and those who don't. . . . And for the kids who don't have the technological skills they'll need to be successful in an ever-more-globalized and technologically driven society, trouble lies ahead.**

Yep, make it happen. Kids are placed into cooperative learning groups of either four, five, or six kids and posed the challenge of making their own 30-second television commercials. Yes, it'll be a lot of fun, but there will be a lot of work, too, and inevitably every group is going to face a lot of challenges.

"So solve them," I say. "Make it happen." This is the mantra I use to push all of my students through.

If you don't have a video camera, borrow one from an uncle, an aunt, or another group. If the sound quality is terrible, go rerecord your commercial and pay particular attention to the audio element of making a video even if you have to get together on a Sunday at 9:00 P.M. to do so. Your battery died, your computer crashed, your mom doesn't want your friends messing up her kitchen—go solve your problems. Make it happen!

The only way to push through, I've found, is to remove the idea from my students' minds that there is a justifiable reason for them not to push through.

Because there isn't. Make it happen.

Actually, the biggest problem I see is usually that one particular group member is lame. "So fire him or her," I say. "Kick the person out of your group and carry the extra weight."

Actually, I have a process in place for firing a group member. First comes a warning, an internal meeting of the group. Then, should the problems continue, comes a consultation with me where I try to intervene and clear the air. If all that doesn't work, groups can either divide into smaller groups or fire individual members, but the newly formed factions thus become responsible for creating their own projects without any extension of the deadline. Sometimes fired individuals must work alone.

I do this because in life we must learn to work well with others, even those people we don't like very much, because if we can't, there will be consequences.

Ultimately, this video project offers all sorts of real-world skills. As I tell my students, we're not just doing a school project for English class in my room; we are making sure everyone in this class possesses a host of other tools they will one day need to survive in the workforce. What I've learned is that when a teacher sets sail to cross the Digital Divide, lots of other important cargo is transported on the boat.

Of course, mayhem ensues. And the first year I did this project with my kids, I was hanging on by the skin of my teeth the whole way through. Outlines, rubrics, storyboards, scripts, costumes, cameras, kids that became megalomaniacs and actresses that became pouty—I juggled it all.

Basically, I invite my students to either invent their own product or use a product that is currently on the market and craft their own commercial for it.

"Mr. Alan, can we do a new kind of Nike sneaker?"

"Yes."

"Mr. Alan, can we invent a product called Homework Go-Away that works like hairspray but gets rid of your math assignments?"

"Yes."

"Yo, Mr. Alan, can we do a commercial on drugs?"

"Uhm . . . no," I replied. "But you can do an antidrug commercial. I'll allow that."

"Cool," my students responded, and off to work they went.

As I told my class, I didn't want to see the commercials. I didn't even really want to know too much about them, other than in broad strokes. This is because I wanted to view their commercials on the due date with open, fresh eyes. Execution mattered much more to me than content.

At least at the time.

"Make it happen," I repeated. "And on the due date, no excuses."

Weekend meetings that lasted for hours were common, but on the due date, everyone showed up that first year with a project. The Nike commercial had wonderful slow-motion effects. The Homework Go-Away was a product that would have made my kids billionaires if they could really have invented such a thing. The antidrug commercial was a pensive, brooding, dark episode that made me realize just how remarkably talented the students in all my classes could be if empowered with the opportunity to stretch themselves. It was wonderful.

Then came the MasterCard commercial.

At the time, there was a TV commercial for the MasterCard credit card that was themed around the idea that in this world, there were some things that money could not buy. And for everything else, there was MasterCard. My students decided to do their own version of this commercial.

"Okay, sure," I thought at the time when they pitched me the project idea. That was all I wanted to know.

The lights were turned off, they inserted their DVD into the player, and the MasterCard commercial began to play.

"A dinner date with the girl in math class . . . thirty-seven dollars."

A video of two of my students, a boy and a girl, on a date leaving a local restaurant while smiling, accompanied the voice-over.

"A movie with a large soda pop . . . twenty-six dollars."

A video of two of my students, the same boy and girl, leaving a movie theater while smiling and holding a large soft drink, accompanied the voice-over.

"An ice-cream cone at a table by the window . . . four dollars."

A video of the same two students laughing and enjoying an ice-cream cone accompanied the voice-over.

The video then cut to the front porch of what was intended to be the girl's house. The scene was set for a goodnight kiss. The students in class started making "woo-woo" noises. Everyone, including myself, was greatly enjoying this commercial.

Then the girl dropped to her knees and disappeared from the picture frame.

"Oral sex on the front porch," said the voice-over. "Priceless."

A big grin crept across the boy's face. Fade to black, commercial over. The lights went on.

At first the crowd erupted with hoots and hollers, but then it quickly got very quiet in my room as all eyes stared at me. I slowly rose from my seat in the audience and walked to my desk. The longer I didn't talk, the more the tension grew.

Soon, everyone began to sense that something was wrong. Very wrong. Anger started to bubble up inside of me.

"Okay, Alan," I said to myself, "count to ten. One, two, three, four. . . ."

"All right, everybody out!" I suddenly shouted.

Thirty-five kids looked at me, entirely bewildered.

"I said out! Now! Everybody! Go to lunch. You're being dismissed twelve minutes early. Go!"

My students started to quickly collect their things.

"Except you five," I said. "You five, stay here."

The people responsible for the MasterCard commercial stood frozen in their tracks as the rest of my class filed quietly past them out the door, shaking their heads and thanking the Lord that they were not part of the group of kids that had obviously crossed the line in Mr. Alan's sand.

"What in the world are you thinking?" I shouted once we were alone in my room. The students were stone silent.

"Rosario," I yelled at the girl with the lead female role in the commercial. "How about if I call up your father and show him this?"

She went white as a ghost.

"Alfred, you're mother is about as churchgoing as they come. What do you say we clue her in on your latest work?"

"I told you it was stupid, Edwin," Alfred said to the ringleader of their crew. Alfred was quaking. In every way, shape, and form, Alfred hadn't been raised like that.

"It's not Edwin's fault," I snapped. "It's yours, Alfred. And yours. And yours, and yours, too!" I said as I went around the circle of culprits. "Each of you played a role in the production of this, and to tell you the truth, you just made an outright mockery of everything we are trying to do in here. And what if the principal had walked in?"

All of them looked down in shame.

"I'm failing you for the project, I'm failing you for the quarter, and I'm going to make sure that each of you is kicked out of the honors program for the blatant dishonor you have shown for this class, this school, and women in general."

Their eyes practically bulged out.

"What, that shocks you? Well, let me tell you something, taking an F on a high school report card is going to look like a bowl of ice cream compared with what going through this world without an education is going to look like if this is how you're going to treat your assignments in high school. But keep screwing around. Keep pretending you don't know that people without diplomas end up in low-wage jobs. Keep pretending you don't know that people without diplomas end up with no health insurance. Keep pretending you don't know that . . . aw, do I even need to go on? I mean, how many times have we gone over this stuff? How many times have I reiterated that, whether you want to admit it or not, right now, as teenagers in an inner-city, Title I school, you're playing for keeps?"

All of them kept their eyes low.

"Education pays, folks, and at this moment, you are stupidly throwing yours away," I said. "And there's just no excuse."

I stared, waiting for some kind of response. None of them even looked up.

"I only hope you make better decisions in the future. Now get out," I said, and without another word, all five of the students left.

From a classroom management perspective, I learned an incredibly valuable lesson that day: always clearly spell things out. I was too cavalier with my students, and by not defining the parameters of the project, by not clearly spelling out the rules of appropriate content and the mandate that anything we showed or did in my room must be appropriate to show to the principal, I'd left room for my teens to push what they thought would be a funny joke into the realm of something that was, in my opinion, incredibly serious.

And so, as casual as I am with my students, I also don't leave anything to their assumptions anymore. If I want to have a classroom rule, maintain a classroom policy, or have any sort of line in the sand, I clearly communicate it. It's a lesson I learned the hard way.

And now when we do propaganda video projects every year, I tell my students the story of the MasterCard commercial. And I haven't had a problem with content ever since.

As it turned out, all five of the MasterCard culprits ended up graduating, and during the final week of senior year, I saw the ringleader in the halls.

"Graduating, huh?" I said with a clear subtext. This student and I would always have the bond of knowing what had happened in my room that day. Though I had forgiven him and, ultimately, did not punish him in a draconian way, it was still something I'd never let him live down.

"Yep, and going to Cal State LA in the fall," he replied.

"College, huh?" I answered. "Nice."

"Got to, Mr. Alan," he said, "because education pays."

I long ago realized that when it comes to classroom management, teens are teens are teens and almost all of them are going to test a teacher's boundaries. However, that day when I blew up at my students, I was walking a very narrow and imprecisely defined line as well. On one hand, I was just a regular ol' teacher preaching to my kids the value of how education in America pays, especially when the deck of cards is already stacked against you.

Yet on the other hand, there was a subtext to my words, too. A subtext that had to do with race.

The truth is, when you teach at a school made up almost exclusively of minority students, many of whom are part of families living at or near the poverty line, it's disingenuous not to acknowledge that there is a role that skin color sometimes plays in American schools and society.

Racial divisions are spectacularly alive in today's United States.

Teach Teens That Education Pays

Let's be honest: I'm a white teacher in an urban school where there are virtually no white students, and while it's never really been an issue of tension between my students and me, my Caucasian-ness definitely comes up. I remember once in class when we were talking about the crooks on Wall Street who lost billions of dollars for publicly owned companies and still ended up with golden parachutes worth hundreds of millions of dollars in severance pay after they were fired, a kid blurted out, "I can't believe these damn white people," but then immediately followed it up by saying, "Oh, no offense, Mr. Alan." The class laughed, I blushed, and then we moved on. That's typically how it goes.

All I can say is that in my room I work hard, as best I can, for race to melt away as an issue that divides people. As my students know (or so I hope), I believe there are many more ways that we're alike as people than we are unalike as races of people, and I do my best to stay focused on those areas. Admittedly, though, it's not true to say my class operates in a manner that is colorblind. Race is just far too vibrantly alive as an issue in everyday America, in and out of school, and for a white teacher like me even to bring up the issue of race as it pertains to academic achievement is very much like approaching a perilous third rail: drift anywhere near it and I could be terminally electrocuted by a force spectacularly greater than me.

Just to write this feels as if I am venturing into deep waters where there is no life raft available should an opportunist pluck my words out of context and stage a Million Man March on Lynwood High. The subject is beyond sensitive—it's fantastically flammable—and as a white teacher of almost exclusively nonwhite students, I know that whenever I bring the topic of race up, it electrifies conversations in dangerous and frightening ways. Even one misconstrued word or implication can hold dire consequences.

However, skirting tough issues related to race and guarding word choice further mucks up an already murky problem, so I'm just going to come right out and say it: there are blatant racial problems in our schools, all races are responsible for them, and we, as a nation, are doing an incredibly poor job of rectifying them. Truly, things need to change because we are currently perpetuating an educational system that creates a societal bifurcation—one that is morally reprehensible and unequivocally terrible for us all.

Not that I have any strong opinions on the matter or anything.

Education has long been regarded as the ladder by which citizens of our country can hoist themselves up and pursue the American dream. However, if the element of fairness in our schools is removed and all kids are not offered the same high-quality education, a great travesty exists that strikes at the core of our nation's most deeply held ideals, and we run the risk of divisiveness at a time in which we need national, global, and humanistic unity more than ever.

Now, I am most certainly not about to argue that inequity in schools is the sole reason for the academic achievement gap between racial subgroups—many factors are at play and a host of elements contribute to the dilemma—but make no mistake, bias in our public school system exists, and it inarguably slices across racial lines.

Based on my observations, though, the causes of the current inequity are more by-products of systemic failures rather than the tangible result of overt policies designed to be explicitly unfair (as they once were). I mean, I know a lot of people in the world of education, and no one I've ever met is twirling his moustache and consciously trying to oppress anyone by setting up laws, schools, methodologies of teaching, and so forth that disempower students based on such things as the color of their skin, their gender, or their socioeconomic status anymore. (And thank goodness!) But yes, admittedly—and shamefully—it very much used to be this way in our schools. Yet I believe our classrooms can do, and need to do, a much better job of serving the needs of *all* our learners.

What we must realize is that America's current population of teenagers, and by extension the educational institutions designed to teach these students, are now among the most diverse in terms of ethnicity, skill level, command of language, and cultural background ever blended together in the history of the planet. (And nowhere is this more true than in California, but as goes California in many ways, so goes the nation a few years later.) And this, of course, causes tremendous systemic challenges when it comes to serving the needs of all students. However, if we continue to deliver an imbalance in the way that services are provided, materials are distributed, and opportunities are offered to this conglomeration of disparate needs, we will ultimately cause irreparable harm to the entire system, not just those who are unevenly or unfairly served.

Morally, ethically, and pragmatically, we must recognize that when some teenagers are offered technology in the classroom, field trips out of the classroom, and a rich academic curriculum that provides depth, breadth, and scope across a variety of academic disciplines in a safe and nourishing environment, while other teenagers in the same city but a few miles away are forced to negotiate overcrowded classrooms, textbooks riddled with graffiti, and chronic violence on campus, pupils from both sides of the educational fence—and society at large—will ultimately lose.

And lose big.

Diversity in our schools can be one of our greatest strengths. It allows for different perspectives, wider viewpoints, and an exciting collage of insights. Yet diversity can also be our Achilles' heel, too, if selective groupings of students are consistently served in an uneven manner. If we attend only to the needs of certain teenagers in our public schools without equitably serving the needs of others, we cripple public education's credibility and do a disservice to society at large.

Simply put, having an education opens doors; not having an education closes them. I realize this. You realize this. But the teenagers whose butts are sitting in the chairs of our schools do not realize this—at least not well enough. Incumbent upon us, therefore, as teachers, leaders, parents, and adults, in an almost unprecedented way is passing this message along.

Now, I meet parents all the time, and truth be told, Lynwood parents treat me very well. They make me feel as if I hold the job of an esteemed professional and, honestly, I am flattered when they go to administration to make sure their younger children are placed in my classes after I've been a teacher to their older kids. Really, there's no higher compliment and I think they know my door is always open to them.

However, one year I met the mother of one of my students after having just read the class assignment shown in Figure 5–1, which was written by her daughter earlier in the week.

I didn't end up saying anything to the mom. Why? Because she showed up to my class drunk herself.

Goodness, the apple doesn't fall far from the tree, does it?

But then, when I shot this parent that disapproving look, the one that said, "I know your dirty little secret," she looked back at me and said something I found to be both pathetic and profoundly insightful at the same time.

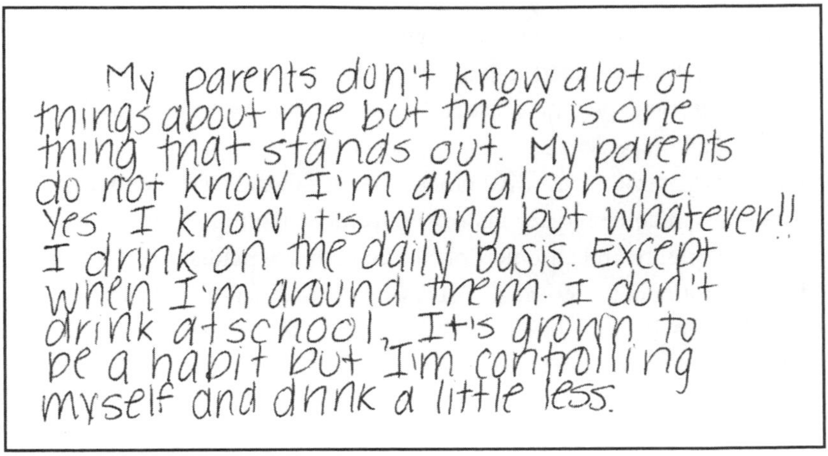

My parents don't know a lot of things about me but there is one thing that stands out. My parents do not know I'm an alcoholic. Yes, I know it's wrong but whatever!! I drink on the daily basis. Except when I'm around them. I don't drink at school, It's grown to be a habit but I'm controlling myself and drink a little less.

Figure 5–1 ● Joanna's Assignment

"You think what you want, but ain't nobody ever told me it was gonna be like this," she offered almost as an excuse for her behavior. "Ain't nobody ever told me it was gonna be like this."

Then she walked out of my room. Though I never saw this woman again, I spent a long time thinking about her words. (And yes, I ended up passing off the information about the student's drinking problem to a school counselor.) For some reason, I found a certain truth in her statement, the kind that people who are all liquored up seem to have a way of speaking.

Now, as we all know, alcohol and drug abuse crosses well beyond skin color, so this is not a race issue I am addressing. However, as we all also know, educational inequity most assuredly exists in our schools and it absolutely slices along racial lines, so I know I'm in a bit of a blurry area right here.

"Was she right?" I kept asking myself. "Did nobody ever tell this African American woman when she was a teenager that it 'was gonna be like this'?" The idea haunted me. "And what did she even mean, 'like this'?"

For the next few days I asked myself these questions over and over again, not letting it go for some reason. Finally, I went back to Joanna (my student) to ask her a few things and discovered that her mother was a high school dropout who first gave birth at the age of 18 and was currently working two part-time jobs. And her father (they were still married, but it most certainly was not an apartment of paradise, Joanna told me) had never really been the type of man to hold a steady job. Soon, after hearing more details about their family's life, I cobbled together a much better insight into what "like this" meant.

"Like this" meant the struggles, the shame, and the perpetual feelings of fiscal and emotional burden one endures when living in poverty. "Like this" meant life was rough, brutally rough.

And unrelenting.

Now, goodness knows I have no desire to cast judgment on Joanna's mother—or anyone who is living under the pressures of an extremely low socioeconomic status—but that day, when the implications of Joanna's mother's visit to my classroom sank in, I vowed that there would never, ever be one of my students who could honestly say to anyone, "Ain't no one ever told me it was gonna be like this" because, guess what . . . I believe someone could have told her.

I believe someone should have told her.

And I believe it's almost criminal not to have told her.

The truth is, a mountain of evidence exists to show that "Yep, based on the choices you made when you were a teenager, a lot of people could have predicted that as a minority African American female in America who gave birth while still a teen without having secured an education, there were a heck of a lot of indicators pointing to things in your life turning out pretty much 'like this.'"

This is now why the first week of my class each and every year isn't filled with silly little icebreaking, get-to-know-you games. No, we jump right into it. I tell my students—and show them—in a straight-out, in-your-face, highly direct manner that "like this" is how it's going to be.

I do it with stats. I do it with data. I do it with cold, dispassionate facts gleaned from the profuse amount of information out there that illuminate exactly what I'm talking about.

Figure 5–2 shows material taken straight from my classroom, stats I show to each and every one of my kids. In my opinion, there's nothing more icy than data. It cuts you to the bone.

It never fails to cast a silent pall over the room when we talk about this stuff because my students often see people they know or are related to reflected directly in the statistics I am showing to them. However, as I tell my kids, this is not me as a white guy standing up on a hill casting

Figure 5–2 🔹 Facts You Need to Know . . .

Facts You Need to Know About How Education Pays

You wanna make a million dollars? Over the course of your lifetime earnings, people with a bachelor's degree will make approximately $1 million more than people who have only a high school diploma.

You wanna make more than a million dollars? Over the course of your lifetime earnings, people with a master's degree will make approximately $1.3 million more than people who have only a high school diploma. (Day & Newburger 2002)

Or maybe you don't like money. . . . A high school dropout earns about $260,000 less than a mere high school graduate over the course of his or her lifetime. (Richard 2005)

Facts You Need to Know About Race and Poverty

Twenty-five percent of African Americans live in poverty.

Twenty-four percent of American Indian and Alaska natives live in poverty.

Twenty-two percent of Latinos/Hispanics live in poverty.

Ten percent of Asian/Pacific Islanders live in poverty.

Nine percent of whites live in poverty.

Twenty-eight percent of all households with no husband present live in poverty.

Thirteen million American children live in poverty (35 percent of all people in poverty are kids; this makes the U.S. first in child poverty in the industrialized world). (Myers-Lipton 2006)

Did you know that 28.4 percent of students between the ages of 5 and 17 years old in Lynwood Unified School District live in poverty? (Snyder, Dillow, & Hoffman 2007)

Figure 5–2 🔹 Facts You Need to Know . . . (Continued)

Facts You Need to Know About Dropping Out of School

One American high school student drops out every nine seconds. Or put another way, 3,000 students a day say hasta la vista to schooling. Gulp! (Martin & Halperin 2006)

The national graduation rate stands at about 68 percent. That means overall, nearly one-third of all public high school students—one out of three—fails to graduate.

But minority graduation rates are woefully lower:

- Blacks graduate approximately 50 percent of the time.

- Hispanics graduate approximately 53 percent of the time.

- Whites graduate approximately 75 percent of the time.

- Asians graduate approximately 77 percent of the time. (Swanson 2004)

- By their mid-30s, 60 percent of black men (six in ten) who had dropped out of school had spent time in prison. (Eckholm 2006)

- More black high school dropouts in their late 20s are in prison (34 percent) than in the workforce (30 percent). (Eckholm 2006)

- Hispanics accounted for 41 percent of all current high school dropouts in 2005. However, they made up only 17 percent of the total youth population. (Child Trends Databank 2005)

- Statistics from Texas show the average prison inmate had a sixth-grade education. (Hendricks, Hendricks, & Kauffman 2001)

Now check out where the money ($$$) goes:

- We spend approximately $80,000 per year, per child, incarcerating juvenile offenders in the state. (Block & Weisz 2004)

- We spend approximately $8,607 per year, per child, educating the children of the state. (Ross 2007) aspersions down on people they know and love but rather my attempt to illuminate for them the fact that they have their own lives, their own choices, and there are options being made available right now that hold severe consequences.

"School is not a punisher," I say. "School is not a jailer. School is not the enemy; rather, it is a chance—a chance *not* to become yet another government statistic like the ones I've just put in front of you."

And if there's one thing true about all teenagers, it's that there's nothing they hate more than the thought of becoming yet another government statistic. (See Appendix I, "Six Tips for Teens to Avoid a Life of Poverty.")

Regardless of race, socioeconomic status, or gender, we must do a better job of teaching our teens that education pays, because over the next hundred years, the gap between those who have an education and those who do not is going to grow so expansive—and disastrous—that we're going to need a whole new series of metaphors to even discuss this chasm.

Lastly (because this could be a book all unto itself), we must do a better job of embracing English language learners. Politics aside, our schools are teeming with students for whom English is not a native tongue, and if we do not find a way to better embrace these pupils, they will continue to reject school as houses of shame and failure—and the negative effects of not better serving the needs of our ELL students hold ramifications for almost every element of our society. For example, consider the projections in Figure 5–3 (Passel & Cohn 2008).

Education must better adapt to the needs of our current population for the sake of everyone involved because it's not just the well educated who will benefit from this; we all will.

Be the person who removes the following words from your kids' mouths: "Ain't nobody ever told me it was gonna be like this."

🌑 Tips for Teaching Teens the Value of Education

Be Blunt

In my opinion, our entire profession needs to be overt, transparent, and incessant about communicating the importance of education because too many kids are simply walking away from our classrooms without understanding the consequences of their laissez-faire decision

Figure 5–3   U.S. Population Projections: 2005–2050

If current trends continue, the population of the United States will rise to 438 million in 2050, from 296 million in 2005.
Eighty-two percent of the increase will be due to immigrants arriving between 2005 and 2050 and their U.S.–born descendants.
Of the 117 million people added to the population during this period because of the effect of new immigration, 67 million will be the immigrants themselves and 50 million will be their U.S.–born children or grandchildren.
Nearly one in five Americans (19 percent) will be an immigrant in 2050.
The Latino population, already the nation's largest minority group, will triple in size and will account for most of the nation's population growth from 2005 through 2050.
It is estimated that Hispanics will make up 29 percent of the U.S. population in 2050, compared with 14 percent in 2005.
The white population will increase more slowly than other racial and ethnic groups.
Whites will become a minority (47 percent) by 2050 [emphasis mine].

to abandon the pursuit of a degree. Additionally, as the world becomes more globalized, this information *does not* apply just to teens of color. White teens without an education are increasingly more outsourced, downsized, laid off, and flat-out screwed if they don't step up and attain high levels of education, too. The ramifications of ignorance apply to all.

Look, I don't want my students to learn this stuff the hard way (which they inevitably will). I want them to learn this while they are still in a strong position to take advantage of their opportunities, before they look out at the circumstances of their lives with remorse. Life is hard enough without being handicapped by the lack of an education. Be candid. Be brusque. Be gruff if need be. Soft-pedaling the issue about the value of being well educated isn't doing anyone in our society (other than the prison builders) any favors.

Teach Teens to Become Active Participants in Their Own Education

Ask teens what their foremost complaint is about school and most of them will respond that there is exceptionally little relevance in the curriculum to their own personal lives. As teenagers quite clearly yap at anyone who will listen (even the ones who are doing well in class blabber on about this), students today just do not feel as if they're being asked to learn things that have authentic, meaningful, purposeful value to them. And as study after study proves, this lack of perceived relevance is the foremost reason that thousands upon thousands of teens every day are saying "sayonara" to our schools and dropping out in droves. (See Figure 5–4.)

Figure 5–4 ● The Top Five Reasons Students Drop Out
(Bridgeland, DiIulio, & Morison 2006)

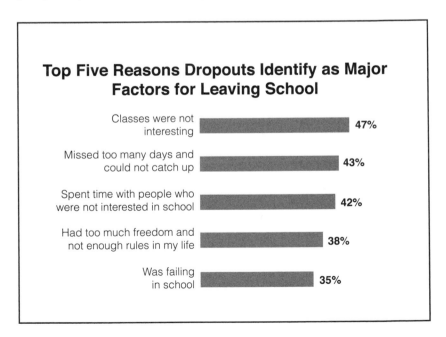

Now, while I very much agree with teens about the fact that our schools are doing a pretty lame job on the "listening and responding to the needs and voices of our students" front, I also strongly believe that by dropping out of high school, teenagers are cutting off their nose to spite their face. Dropping out is a childish, immature, intellectually ill-advised decision based in naïveté and lack of forethought. Truly, the way teens today react to their perceived lack of relevance in the curriculum smacks more of petulance than reasonableness. Look, sometimes people are required to do stuff that isn't all about glee, glamour, glory, and good times.

It's called life.

Sorry kids, but as much as I blast schools for being antiquated and not in touch with your ever-developing needs, the fact is that the problem of relevance in our schools is one to be shared. Really, why is it solely the teacher's job to make education pertinent?

The answer is *it's not!* And in my heart of hearts, I deeply believe that many of today's teens need to get off their butts and start better accepting the fact that they have a role in the classroom, too. People mistakenly assume that just because I believe so earnestly in an engaging curriculum that I, for some reason, don't also fully expect teens to approach their education with abundant enthusiasm.

Nonsense! I have no tolerance whatsoever for kids who believe that they have the God-given right to abdicate their own share of responsibilities when it comes to earning an education. Matter of fact, if I had to take sides, I'd say it's more the kids' job to become well educated than the responsibility of the teacher to forge well-educated students. Why? Because, at the end of the day, the kids have the most to lose.

That's right, the kids. It's why they need to become active participants in school themselves. Indisputably, they have *way* more on the line, which is why when the issue of finding the relevance in school comes up in my own classroom, I completely shift the responsibility from the shoulders of me as the teacher to those of the students. Becoming educated is an active process; it takes not only teachers "doin' their thang" but learners doing what they need to do on their end, too. This is why when my own students gripe about how *boring* their classes are, I tell them to quit whining, grow up, and get with the program.

"Dude, you want relevance, go seek it yourself. School is a two-way street, so don't just sit there waiting for Lynwood High to make something happen. . . . Go make something happen for yourself!"

As I am sure you can imagine, they love hearing that.

However, what I explain to all my kids is that American high schools are very much like self-service gas stations nowadays: teenagers can most certainly fill up their tanks, but "Yo, you better get out and pump!"

I tell my students all the time, "If your approach to becoming educated is sitting back and waiting for someone to come around and remove the nozzle for you, check your tire pressure, top off your fluids, and fill up your educational gas tank, goodness gracious, you're going to be waiting a heck of a long time."

"You want an education," I tell them. "It's out there. Go get it! Some kids who had their butts in the very same seats yours are in right now have gone off to some of the finest universities in America, so zip it and go do something productive for yourself."

Becoming well educated, earning a degree, and attaining the benefits of a diploma require a heck of a lot of effort *from the student's side of the desk.* The it-takes-two-to-tango motif of school is irrefutable. Matter of fact, I believe that students should always be working much harder than the teacher is at the front of the room. Unfortunately, our current classrooms have the expectations about this dynamic all flipped around. Really, it's almost laughable; teens today expect the teachers to do more work, expend more effort, and care more deeply about the students' educations than the kids do themselves.

Nonsense.

I don't care what color a kid's skin is, how much of a jerk the dad is, or how high the odds are stacked against the student before the kid walks into my classroom. Teens today must learn that attaining an education is their own responsibility and if they want relevance, if they want value, if they truly have a desire for knowledge, it is most certainly out there. But they are going to have to go out and find it for themselves!

Teens must be active learners. The sooner they learn this, the better off they'll be.

Watch for the Three Enemies of Embracing the Value of Education

Arbitrary Time Frames

I know a teacher—a Teacher of the Year award winner, as a matter of fact—who was a solid D student back when he was in high school. Now, he's a 45-year-old man who teaches elementary science in a Title I school where he has impoverished, blind students building rocket launchers in a wholly original standards-based, project-based educational curriculum he's designed all by himself to the kudos of everyone who has ever seen him work.

But he once had a teacher who believed in him.

Antonio Villaraigosa, the current mayor of the city of Los Angeles, was once a high school dropout who eventually returned to class, clawed his way into UCLA, and went on to an accomplished career in public service.

But he once had a teacher who believed in him.

The story of how just one teacher can change a person's whole life is literally a cliché. (A good one though.) Yet sometimes society has arbitrary time frames set in place that really cause more problems than they provide solutions. So what if a kid isn't a whiz at math by the age of 13? Who cares if biology isn't the most fascinating subject to a 15-year-old girl with a cell phone blowin' up with text messages? Einstein didn't speak until he was 5, Colonel Sanders didn't start serving chicken until he was in his 60s, and on and on and on. There are many late bloomers in this world and just because some 14-year-olds aren't grasping the significance of their world history class doesn't mean that the world is over for them.

Remember, it's not over when you fail; it's over when you give up. Don't apply arbitrary time-frame expectations to kids who are struggling. They might just need a few more moments.

The Negative Ramifications of Going Against the Tide

Goodness knows when this happened, how it became institutionalized, or how we can alter the entire psyche of a generation, but the fact is that being smart, acting intelligently, and doing well in school carries the very real chance of social stigma for today's teens that often results in kids being ostracized for doing well in school.

As a result, many kids are sabotaging themselves. They lay low, they don't try hard, they don't raise their hands to give answers in class, nor do they hungrily pursue their own education because of social pressure. Girls won't give their best out of concern for what boys might think, bullies who don't do well on quizzes rule the playground with unmitigated terror, causing intelligent kids to repress their studious ways out of fear, and dysfunctional families have parents or older relatives who often seek to undermine teens from attaining levels of academic achievement that they themselves never had the guts or gumption enough to go for in their own lives.

While I have no idea how to purge this from the mentality of society, in my own class I have found that it helps to tell the metaphorical story about crabs in a pot.

When crabs are caught by fishermen they are tossed into open, uncovered pots. What's interesting is that crabs actually have the ability to scale the walls and climb out of these pots, but they rarely do. Why? It's not for lack of trying—crabs desperately claw all the time. Rather, the reason they rarely escape is because once one crab starts to move upward, the other crabs down below yank it back down.

And then when another crab climbs up, they bring that one back down, too, until finally all the crabs end up being trapped together so no one gets out alive.

It's the ultimate zero-sum game causing everyone to lose.

Rather than pretend the taunts that come with doing well in school do not exist, we should bring the issue out in the open for teens because, as I always tell my own class, you may get teased and taunted for being a nerd, a brain, or a teacher's pet, but if you think of those who are doing it through the prism of knowing how crabs trapped in a pot behave, it's a lot easier to forge on and accomplish your own individual dreams.

Teach teens to think for themselves, do what's in their own best interests, and go against the tide.

Telling Teens What You Want Them to Do
Instead of Respecting What It Is They Want to Do

The audacity we in education demonstrate by trying to box our teens into an ever-narrowing paradigm that meets our own desires for them much to the exclusion of listening to their desires for themselves smacks of spectacular arrogance and does a disservice to us all. Really, in my class I don't care if my students want to become computer programmers, musicians, auto mechanics, molecular geneticists, beauty shop owners, or airline pilots because hey, we need all of these professions—and many, many more—going forward. But what we especially need are people who really want to do these jobs, not a bunch of people who just sort of end up in these positions by default by not having the skills necessary to go out and do something else about which they'd be much more passionate.

Look, no one's gonna cure cancer with a punchin'-the-clock, 9-to-5 mentality. As many teachers know, when it comes right down to it . . .

YOU GOTTA WANNA!

Our job is not to judge teens' interests but rather to empower students with the ability to fully pursue their interests while teaching them the basic life skills they'll need to navigate the demands of society.

This is why cutting music programs, pulling back from vocational ed, shrinking elective courses, and narrowing the curriculum is a terrible trend that needs to be reversed. In many ways ours teens are learning in spite of our schools. Avoid telling teens what you want them to do instead of respecting what it is they want to do.

6

Making the Mix Match
Teaching Teens to Go Where Their Inner Fire Burns

Some of my students come from solid, middle-class homes. They live with two parents, regularly visit the mall, and take family vacations to places like the Grand Canyon.

> I will cite three things I did over Spring Break. First, I went to the Grand Canyon with my family. We did a lot of "hiking," although I'd like to consider it as Extreme Hiking. After, we went to Laughlin. My parents went to the casino, while I went to the arcade... we all lost money happily. The last was a trip to the mall. My friends and I rode a carousel.

> Over Spring Break, I did three enjoyable things. Shopping comes first. It was fun being able to spend time with some of my friends looking for a cute outfit. My trip to UCLA comes next. I had an incredible day with my sister after not seeing her for three weeks. My family reunion comes last. I spent time with my family and caught up with my cousins I don't get to see often.

And some of them don't.

> It started when I was little, I saw someone get shot in front of my house. In elementary school a man pointed his gun at my face.
> Then in Middle school there were a lot of gangs, drugs, and money. Be dangerous to be out late at night

> Gangs also affect my family really bad. Their always stealing stuff from us like bikes, cars and even little stuff like basketballs and stuff. One day there was a driveby right in front of my house while me and my buddy were playing Xbox. At first I thought it was fireworks but once I heard another shot along with a breaking window I ran for cover. I the past year There has been over 5 shooting on my block. Now everyday when I walk outside J think to myself, "What will happen today?" and I'm hoping that I don't get shot. Now that all these shootings are happening im actually kind of terrified to walk the streets alone or walk to school

How am I supposed to react when I read student writing such as this? How am I supposed to hold these students accountable to the same expectations I hold for all my students when these kids are clearly facing things outside of class that not all other students are facing, things that will most assuredly have an impact on their in-class performance? And how much can I really be expected to accomplish in just 55 minutes a day with teens like these when they are so often hamstrung by patchy attendance, a lack of well-educated role models in their circle of everyday interpersonal interactions, and an unstable (and frequently stressful) home life?

I love teaching at Lynwood High, but there are moments when it scalds my heart. Simply put, sometimes I just don't know what to do or where to begin when faced with all these challenges.

The fact is that 28.4 percent of all students between the age of 5 and 17 years old in the Lynwood Unified School District live in poverty (Snyder, Dillow, & Hoffman 2007). *Poverty!* This means that almost 30 percent of my students go home to concerns like the electricity being turned off, eviction notices for their families, and questions about how much food is on the table or clothing is on their backs. Tough to do homework with a belly that growls for grub.

My students don't just come to class with varying degrees of skill sets in the realm of academic performance; they enter my room with an entirely vast and disparate spectrum of emotional needs, personal histories, and family influences on their scholastic attitudes and behaviors. Additionally, many of them have varying commands of the English language, different levels of access to resources such as technology and school supplies once they leave campus, and a host of different prisms through which they even view the idea of what school can mean to their lives.

Some teens view high school in a manner that makes them easy to teach; they're eager to learn and excited to one day go to college. For others, school is a cross between a social club, a fashion show, and a dating game. Friends take precedence over homework, study habits, and the SAT. Still others view school as a curse, an institution of confinement, a place they simply can't wait to leave as soon as the opportunity presents itself. They hate school and, in their minds, school hates them. Most kids, though, are a mix-and-match conglomeration of all three schools of thought at various times during their teenage years. My job is to view *all* my students with compassion and determine every student's individual capacities so I can individualize my teaching practice—and this while they arrive in groupings of 35 at a time at my doorstep during a stage of their lives when they are undergoing bursts of puberty.

And of course I'm supposed to do all of this while keeping accurate attendance records, finding my own resources, and praying that the photocopy machine is functioning when I need it. Goodness, a person could go cuckoo just thinking about it.

Obviously, crafting a classroom so that I can teach in a way that best adapts to the unique needs, capacities, and learning styles of each of my students is a tremendous challenge. However, it's a task made more manageable when I remind myself that our public schools take on all comers.

While I do think it's appropriate to view education somewhat as though we are running a business in which our students are our customers and our job is to serve them with the best intellectual nourishment we can provide (the mentality that I work for the kids is very much a theme throughout my day), school is also very different from a business. For example, if a supplier sends a restaurant a moldy crate of vegetables, the restaurant will refuse to accept or pay for them and will send the vegetables back with the expectation that new, fresh vegetables will replace the inadequate first offering. And if not, the restaurant will seek another supplier for its produce. Our public schools, though, accept all students, regardless of who they are, where they come from, or whether they even want to be sitting in our classrooms.

And we take them as they are.

Therefore, when tenth-grade students enter my room with fifth-grade literacy levels, I don't get mad at the kids for being inadequate. I don't punish or shame them for not being at the level of academic proficiency where they "should" be. Rather, I simply take kids where they are and work diligently at trying to improve their abilities. While there is absolutely no excuse for a student to enter tenth grade using a lowercase i to write a sentence such as "i went to the store" (something I see far more than I ever expected I would—and not just in the essays my English language learners turn in), I know that if I allow myself to dwell on my negative emotions when I see these types of elementary school errors in high school, it will detract from my ability to do what it is I've been hired to do: teach.

Ultimately, it becomes a matter of mind-set. As the Hebrews say, "Some boatmen curse the lack of wind; others row." (At the end of the year, though, no kid ever leaves my room using the lowercase i to write "I went to the store," small triumph that this may be.)

Unfortunately, though, lots of educators do bemoan their students' low skills, as if being deficient of academic aptitude is something the kid is personally doing to teachers in order to torture them and make their life as educators miserable. Me, I empathize. Really, what student who has language arts skills five years below grade level doesn't already know it, doesn't want to hide it, and doesn't already feel ashamed of it? And knowing what the future may hold for some of these kids if they don't turn their academic steamships around, I know they need an ally, not an adversary. To meet the needs of all my learners, then, I must remain compassionate.

Another thing I do is to make sure I focus on finding out what my kids *can* do, instead of just identifying what they *can't*—especially at the beginning of the year when I am first establishing my relationships with the students in my class. For the first two months in my room I even have a personal credo I try to follow: do not write anything that is not positive or encouraging on a student's paper.

Nothing. For the entire first two months. And guess what? In all the time since I've adopted this policy, never has there been an instance when I have looked down at a kid's work and said to myself, "There's not a damn nice thing I can say right now. This is pathetic!"

And why's that? Well, it's not because I haven't gotten some outrageously awful student work, I'll tell you that much. Nope, it's because I

> " When tenth-grade students enter my room with fifth-grade literacy levels, I don't get mad at the kids for being inadequate. I don't punish or shame them for not being at the level of academic proficiency where they "should" be. Rather, I simply take kids where they are and work diligently at trying to improve their abilities.

know that if I am reading a paper, it means a student actually did something for me in the first place and while that may not sound like a lot, there are many teachers in schools like mine across the country who don't even get that much out of their kids. Truly, our nation is plagued with legions of teenagers who won't do squat for their teachers in school, kids who are but one more harsh teacher's comment away from dropping out on the very first day that they show up to class, so I don't want to do anything to push my new kids over the edge. No, there will be plenty of time to break out my red pen later in the school year, but for the first two months of school, adhering to my pledge to avoid negative comments helps me build the trust I am going to need to really be effective later on while simultaneously allowing me to see my students for who they often are: struggling learners who need help, not castigation.

Besides, with as much as I know about the plight of our public schools today, isn't ripping into teens for their low academic abilities at the start of the school year when they first enter my class a bit like blaming the victim?

All students are different, all students learn at their own pace, and all students learn in their own way, and if I hold unreasonable expectations for my students before they even enter my room and demonstrate what they can do—as opposed to solely looking for what they cannot—I don't think I'm being fair to the child. For me, it's pretty clear-cut: build 'em up, don't break 'em down; apply patience, elbow grease, and compassion, then take it from there.

After all, before they build skyscrapers, they engineer solid foundations.

Most significantly, though, I am perpetually striving to have my students look in their hearts and pursue areas of study they're passionate about, for it is my belief that inside a student's greatest interests lie a teacher's greatest educational opportunities.

I teach teens to go where their inner fire burns. In life, passion can be the ultimate equalizer.

Teach Teens to Go Where Their Inner Fire Burns

Modern-day education baffles me. I mean, I'm a teacher and I love the classroom, but truly, some of the things going on in our schools today challenge all common sense.

And I know for a fact I'm not the only person who feels this way.

Considering that I'm an English teacher, I'll make a point of explicating the ridiculousness of our nation's math curriculum first. (And you thought I was above petty departmental rivalry . . . *Ha!*)

For example, it makes no sense that although 99 percent of teenagers will never have to determine the value of x degrees in an isosceles triangle after they leave high school, we continuously and obstinately deny kids their high school diplomas if they can't answer two-dimensional geometrical conundrums cooked up by highfalutin test makers who work in think tanks far removed from the flesh-and-blood, day-to-day interactions with actual teens.

Uh, hello? Why is geometry a mathematical gatekeeper to the doors of high school graduation? (To wit, check the graduation requirements of practically every high school in America; no geometry credits, no diploma. Or, for states such as mine, with a high school exit exam, there is a math section that clearly demands knowledge of geometry, and if you don't pass this test, you don't get a diploma.) Me, I haven't used my isosceles skills once since I was 17 years old.

Honestly, when was the last time you calculated the measurements of opposing angles inside a parallelogram?

If we are going to mandate math for every teen in the country (and I do think we ought to), shouldn't we make part of our essential curriculum revolve around the principles of money? After all, 100 percent of teens are going to need to know about cash at some point in their lives, about how to manage it, save it, invest it, spend it, borrow it, and budget it. Financial literacy helps people escape poverty, shows them how to navigate the inevitable fiscal demands of running a home, and empowers folks to set themselves up for a prosperous and fulfilling future. Will somebody please show me how knowledge of secondary-level geometry trumps the vital importance of that? And please don't feed me the line that says geometry teaches critical thinking. Sure, I'll grant that it does, but this is a by-product of learning geometry, not the primary objective or focus, and if the goal of our schools in mandating geometry to graduate is that students learn how to think critically then we should, indeed, teach a class on critical thinking, something that includes the direct instruction of the subject such as solving logical-reasoning puzzles, playing chess, filling in sudoku boxes, whatever. But geometry on its own? As my friends in the South would say, "That dog just don't hunt."

Now obviously I don't want to bite the hand that feeds me in our school system by saying the emperor of education has no clothes, but guess what? THE EMPEROR OF EDUCATION HAS NO CLOTHES!

Really, who's in charge of this asylum? At best, most high school math classes are tangentially correlated to real-world skills that students will eventually need. At worst, they are entirely irrelevant. After all, I left high school prepared to circumcise a rhomboid, but darn if it helped me not to get suckered into an introductory teaser offer that later ballooned to a 30 percent interest rate on my first shiny credit card.

Es muy ridiculo! as the Spanish would say. (Yep, those very same Spanish who struggle to read the geometrical word problems on these high-stakes tests because they are English language learners who get no special accommodations made for them.)

Now don't get me wrong, I'm all for making sure that students eat their intellectual vegetables (i.e., learn the essential skills they need to know to later thrive in the workforce, in life, etc.), but in a lot of classes, these aren't meat and potatoes we're serving; they are side dishes being falsely propagandized as key intellectual ingredients on the academic food pyramid.

What we really need to do is lay our nation's entire scholastic program on the table, look at each and every component, and ask, "Why are we teaching this?" And then, once we separate the wheat from the chaff—and trust me, there is chaff—we need to reconfigure our schools to authentically meet the needs of twenty-first-century students in light of our reevaluation. Making it universally obligatory that a teen learns such things as the process of mitosis, how to identify gerund phrases in passages coldly plucked from larger readings, and key facts about the Hundred Years' War between England and France in the year 1337 in order to earn their diploma may have been tucked under the umbrella of essential knowledge back in the twentieth century (though how, I am still not sure), but in this day and age, these arenas of education, while certainly having legitimacy, no longer seem justifiable as core, know-it-or-you-don't-get-a-diploma studies.

I'll try to put this delicately: It's time for a spring cleaning!

As most people who work in schools and most teens who attend them already know, we are way overdue for an Internal Revenue Service–style audit of our curricular reasoning. Of course, the real problem that lies at the heart of this whole quandary stems from one true problem: our one-size-fits-all approach to education.

One-size-fits-all schooling makes no sense. It doesn't allow for varying learning styles, it doesn't take into account various intellectual strengths, and it doesn't accommodate a range of dispositional proclivities.

I'll grant that in certain cases, one size really does fit all. Obviously, all students need to have a strong, solid, core base of essential knowledge regardless of where their interests lie in order to function and thrive in society. All kids need to be able to read. All kids need to be able to do basic math. All kids need to be able to write. It's called the three Rs. (*Note:* This is not an original theory.)

And our schools *must* teach these things (and we must improve our teaching of them as well.)

However, while there is a place for geometry, mitosis, gerund phrases, and so forth, these skills should not be prerequisites to high school graduation because the philosophy that makes them so is creating huge rifts in our ability to effectively educate today's students. See, when teens refuse to learn the academic material we mandate that they absorb under the disingenuous guise of it being essential (because they know it is *not*), and we don't let them learn other skills they find to be more useful, relevant, appealing, and valuable to graduates, they begin to doubt our intellectual leadership. We, as their educators, then lose credibility with our students, who—understandably so—begin to drift.

And tune out.

And, as we see increasingly these days, teens are just simply dropping out, which creates a cascade of societal problems that are almost inevitably tied back to their not having some sort of education that could have well served them to meet the demands of life in the first place. (Crime, poverty, welfare, limited income ability—there's a direct link to all of them from a lack of education.)

Clearly, we've backed ourselves into a corner of educational dysfunction—and our own faulty logic as to what is essential in the world of diplomas is the primary culprit. Unfortunately, our curriculum, instead of strengthening us, is now oppressing us. The simple fact is the world has changed and our schools have not kept pace.

Therefore the question really becomes how, in this wi-fi, hip-hop, where-has-all-the-sanity-gone world, can a teen better navigate and survive our nation's off-base academic policies?

In my opinion, it begins and ends with encouraging teens to follow a path where their inner fire burns. Passion counts more than ever.

When I first became an educator, I was indoctrinated into a system of schooling that implied that teaching kids to pursue matters about which they were enthusiastic was a touchy-feely type of methodology that needed to take a backseat to teaching the more tangible (and testable) skills of English class such as dissecting the subtext of a narrative poem or identifying the use of figurative language. It was as if liking what you were doing was some sort of luxury in school. Nowadays I am of the exact opposite opinion.

In order for students' work to shine—not just make the grade but rise to a level where the quality is supreme—kids must care about what they are doing. This is an absolute. Who is really going to argue the fact that teenagers work best when they are energized and excited by their pursuits? And, by extension, can we not, as educators, then expect better results and more productivity from teens simply because of the fact that they are enthusiastic about what they are studying?

Of course we can. It's a proverbial win-win situation.

Unfortunately, though, you can't *make* a person passionate about anything. Zeal can't be legislated. Yet (lucky for us) an inner fire most assuredly burns in the heart of every teen. And it can be tapped. (And if you don't think so, you don't know teens very well.) In my own classroom, the classic biographical research paper exemplifies this point.

As an English teacher I know I'm dead in the water if I mandate that my students write a five-paragraph essay about Martin Luther King. Not that there's anything wrong with Dr. King, but I've learned the hard way (through piles of listless papers) that kids don't want to do research on people whom *I* find interesting; they want to research people whom *they* find interesting. Nowadays, therefore, when I assign the biographical research paper, I allow my students to choose their own subjects of interest—and yep, sure enough, I get papers about people like Kurt Cobain, Bob Marley, and Jay-Z. However, I also get assignments that are heartfelt, thorough, detailed, and delivered with genuine spark—all while demonstrating a solid knowledge of the same skills I would have sought to teach using MLK as the subject of the paper (i.e., theme, structure, vivid vocabulary, argumentative evidence, a bibliography of sources in MLA style, etc.). And though it may sound antithetical to what most people expect from kids who are doing mere classroom work, the assignments my teens turn in to me for projects framed through this type of student-centered methodology frequently exceed the minimum requirements of the original task and are quite often first-rate. Students, when given a degree of self-directed learning and strongly encouraged to pursue an area of genuine meaning to their own interests (i.e., something that they, as free-thinking individuals, want to say), will almost always bring a sense of depth, breadth, and scope to their work, which I cannot mandate they produce regardless of how much I threaten or cajole.

You just can't buy intrinsic motivation. It's too authentic, too meaningful, and too real—especially when bubbling through the veins of a teenager. (Goodness, could you imagine what would happen if we could bottle the molecular energy generated by a high school girl? We'd put the entire caffeine industry out of business!)

It's just nuts that we don't heed the fact that the wi-fi, hip-hop teenagers of today long to have their own individual, unique interests and voices validated. One look at the immense popularity of social networking sites is all the proof we should need. Kids who won't spend a lick of time writing a mere three-sentence paragraph for English class have no trouble typing

3,000 words over the course of a seven-hour evening in their online worlds of revel. This is why getting teens to gravitate toward their own passions is so essential. It's where they will try harder, show more enthusiasm, take greater ownership over their efforts, and produce superior-quality work.

When teens are passionate, they deliver better results.

When teens are passionate, they are more willing to overcome obstacles.

When teens are passionate, they frequently show a previously absent willingness to go the extra mile to deliver meaningful performance.

All in all, when teens are passionate, they not only give more to their assignments but get more from doing them, too.

The hard truth is that in our cookie-cutter, one-size-fits-all system of education, finding and following one's passion is really the only defense against an impersonal, faceless, try-to-put-you-in-a-box school system that almost makes victims of its students. Schools these days pound kids with drill-and-kill exercises as if the pot of educational gold at the end of the classroom rainbow is a high standardized test score in a narrowly constricted realm of academic content. But kids don't care about state tests. Truly, even my top students roll their eyes when it's time for the alphabet soup of testing to begin. This is because it holds no internal value to them. The rewards are (and that's assuming that there are some rewards, a mighty big leap) extrinsic at best. Not only is our thinking as to what is essential folly, so is our assessment of it.

Unfortunately, exacerbating the matter even further is the fact that our schools treat the inner drives of teenagers as if they are a problem to be overcome rather than potential we can tap to help our teens develop and grow as people. This is the great misstep of contemporary education. Desire is a source of energy, a passion-generating furnace from which people draw creativity, determination, and *oomph*. When we encourage teens to pursue their inner fires, it works out better for everyone involved—the students, the teachers, the schools, and society.

We can do better and, yes, we need to revamp America's curriculum, but what you can do right now is make sure that your teens are looking into their hearts and discovering the things they find personally meaningful. If teens don't like exploring the inner workings of nuclei, let it go. However, if teens are intrigued by the process of looking through microscopes at the matters that make up matter, then empower them to move all the way up the line to becoming a molecular geneticist if that sort of stuff winds their clock. But despite what the powers that be in America would have you think, not everyone needs to become a human genome mapper. I mean, heaven forbid my car breaks down on my way home from school, I am going to sit by the side of the road until someone who can make my carburetor start to carb again tows me to a person who knows how to fix it. (Auto mechanics is not my forte, as you can see . . . but so what?)

Yet, do we have to build a societal system in which the mechanics who fix my engine are trapped in low-paying jobs because they were never given the skills, encouragement, or validation in school to one day own their own auto repair shops? It just does not make any sense.

Renowned psychologist Abraham Maslow told us years ago that high achievers are driven by more than just their skills; they are driven by their internal fires. The only people who prepare great meals are people who like to cook. The only people who write great stories are people who like to write. The only people who create great computer games, give outstanding massages, or grow award-winning roses are people who like to create computer games, give massages, or grow rose bushes. Encourage your teens to reach for what they like to do because the only people who ever truly make it to the top, from Einstein to Mother Teresa to Michael Jordan, are people who were motivated over and above everything else by their own passions for doing the work.

> "
> Our schools treat the inner drives of teenagers as if they are a problem to be overcome rather than potential we can tap to help our teens develop and grow as people. This is the great misstep of contemporary education.

Tips for Teaching Teens to Follow Their Passions

Identify, Think, and Excavate

Any time I see a house being built on an empty lot, I know that somewhere, somebody has a set of plans that were created before construction began. Whether there will be two bathrooms or four, whether there'll be an attic or a cellar, whether the bedrooms will have large closets or small, all decisions were thought out long before anyone started pounding nails.

So how come when our teens embark on building something as monumentally important as their lives, we in the schools don't overtly emphasize the significance of seriously thinking about the type of life they'd like to build for themselves before we set them free in the wild blue yonder? Mostly, we just give students a bunch of random tools—a saw, some nails, a screwdriver, a few isosceles triangle skills—and tell them *good luck and bon voyage*. Is it any wonder so many people in this country just seem to end up in jobs that they don't really care for and merely do because they need to pay the bills?

Let's encourage our teens to discover their authentic inner interests and think about the type of house they'd one day like to build for themselves before they leave our classrooms. Let's provide guidelines so they can be purposeful and thoughtful as they work to discover what moves them. Yes, it can be messy, even abstract, imprecise, and obtuse at some points, particularly at the start for many teens, but most students already have a sense of the things in which they are deeply interested. And sure, some will try to hide behind the claim that they have no idea what it is that they like, but this is quickly dealt with by telling teens, "It's okay not to know; it's not okay, however, not to search."

Identify, think, unearth, and excavate. Really, there is little sense in having people begin construction on something until they know what it is they hope to create. The answers are there for teens; it's just that sometimes they're buried. Have teens dig.

Get Teens to Listen to Their Individual Inner Voice

Yes, our own unique, individual passions are the best foundation for building a fulfilling and rewarding life, but often teens have spent so much time listening to the directions, orders, mandates, and suggestions of others that they don't even know how to clear the fog of other people's ideas from their heads so that they can clearly think for themselves to arrive at authentic answers as to what it is that they personally like and would like to pursue.

In my experience, the process of figuring out the answers is often best assisted through writing. When we write things down, we are forced to make decisions that more clearly allow us to see what it is we really think. Whether it's creating a list, brainstorming a host of possibilities, doodling on a mind map, or using any one of a hundred different graphic organizers, the process of sorting out authentic inner interests for teenagers is almost always strengthened by putting pen to paper.

Have teens work it out by writing it down.

Reserve Judgment About Their Choices

What teen doesn't want to be a rock 'n' roll superstar? (Heck, I still want to be one.) But just because many kids can't play a lick of electric guitar doesn't mean that they still might not be able to one day work in the profession of rock and roll. Bands need managers, roadies, and agents. Recording companies need lawyers, talent scouts, and accounting departments. And between all the limos, hotels, and airplanes, somewhere along the line rock 'n' rollers are going to need a great travel agent, too. Remember, allowing teens to follow their inner fire about an area of deep personal interest to them is really about allowing them to walk through a variety of doors of possibility that might very well lead to new and different doors of possibility one day.

Or even windows. Really, who knows?

🌸 Watch for the Three Enemies of Following Your Passions

Discouragers

Many people are discouragers, and while the reasons for this are as varied as the ways to cook chicken, the simple truth is teens need to know that, unfortunately, not everyone is going to be supportive of whatever path they choose to follow. From parents to teachers to uncles and even friends, experience tells me it's always better to make sure teens know ahead of time that not all folks are going to be sympathetic to them or their choices. In fact, some people will be downright dispiriting.

Complicating this a bit is that teenagers tend to look for the validation of others before pursuing any sort of path. Of course, this makes following one's own inner fire more challenging. Nevertheless, teens must come to learn that seeking external validation to justify their own internal areas of interest is inevitably going to be a recipe for conflict and disillusionment. No, it's most certainly not easy to listen to one's heart, but it is almost always the best compass teenagers have for navigating their lives. (Why we don't teach more teenagers this in school is beyond me. As a farmer in Oklahoma once said, "Happy cows produce good milk.") Teenagers who want to be pastry chefs shouldn't go to medical school because it's what their mothers want. Choices such as those rarely work out well.

Shame Associated With Changing Paths

The process of discovering where one's inner fire burns is not always straightforward. Sometimes teens will discover that what they thought they wanted has turned out to be something that they very much do not want once they've learned more about it.

That's okay.

As a matter of fact, it's more than okay; it's to be saluted. There is no shame in changing directions. Truly, it's what most accomplished people have done at some point in their lives.

Of course, society perpetuates the incorrect assumption that successful people start off life having chosen one fixed direction and then blaze their way to direct success, but the truth is most successful people have zigzagged their way to the top. They most often have followed a very back-and-forth, up-and-down pattern whereby they imagined, conceptualized, identified, plotted, acted, reflected, absorbed feedback, made adjustments, acted again, reflected again, absorbed feedback again, readjusted—yet again—and then repeated and repeated and repeated until they finally arrived at a point of genuine accomplishment. This description is a much more accurate picture of how the cycle of real achievement in this world works.

Changing paths to pursue new ambitions is natural. It's the people who do not change, who do not listen to their own hearts, who inevitably have far more trouble later in life.

Shifts are natural; change is good.

Loneliness

Despite the fact that I teach in a school where thousands upon thousands of teens walk through the halls five days a week, each and every one of them completely understands the feeling of being all alone on campus. That's because loneliness is not a physical sensation but rather an emotional one, and when teenagers pursue their own internal passions, they might very well discover that they have to leave the comfort of friends and groups behind. It's tough to do, especially if those teens are the only ones in their crowd who find things like developing black-and-white photos more exciting than going to the mall.

Marching to the beat of your own drummer may sound exciting and energizing on paper, but it takes bravery to follow the interests of your heart. Indeed, even though the rewards frequently last a lifetime, sometimes it's tough; it may even mean giving up old friends who are no longer part of your drive to embrace your passion.

Be clear about the fact that pursing one's inner fires can sometimes be an isolating experience, yet nothing will be more rewarding.

Tell your teens what famed author and teacher Joseph Campbell always advised his own students: "Follow your bliss!"

Preparing for the Unpreparable
Teaching Teens to Take Ownership

7

The cardinal rule that all teachers have to know if they are going to be successful in the modern-day classroom is to be prepared.

Be prepared.

Be ready for the photocopy machine to go down on the day you need to make copies for your big exam, be in possession of a backup strategy when the buses don't show up for your field trip despite the fact that they were booked months in advance and you have nonrefundable theater tickets for 200 students, and be ready for the fact that your substitute teacher will choose, in some unique show of infinite wisdom, to ignore your fantastically well-detailed lesson plan that took you an hour to write and instead decide to let your kids play the card game *Slap!* for the entire day you are out.

Be prepared for it all. And more. Have a plan B, have a plan C, and have a plan D, because when you're a teacher in modern-day America, Murphy's law is often the law of the land. I can't say it enough. Always be prepared!

And though being prepared for anything to happen is a lesson I learned the hard way (each of the previous examples has happened to me), a teacher must also keep in mind the second cardinal rule of being an educator in modern-day America.

As prepared as you try to be, you'll never be able to be prepared for some of the things that actually happen. I know I wasn't.

Maria earned an A each semester of her sophomore year in my English class. She was diligent and studious, and, while not the most outgoing, she certainly wasn't a social outcast either. Though I did not see her much during her junior year, at the start of her senior year, Maria became an AVID (Advancement via Individual Determination) tutor for me. (In my AVID class I incorporated a big-brother-style mentoring system, having older students guide younger students and assist with their classwork, model college-bound behavior, tell my younger kids the real scoop on how to get through Lynwood High and matriculate to college.) Anyway, Maria had the grades, she had the smarts, and she had the desire to give back, the three skills I look for each year when selecting upperclassmen to help my younger teens. Along with a select few other former students, I brought Maria on board to help me with a somewhat drifting group of sophomores I was charged with molding into college-bound, high-achieving, academically hungry scholars.

Obviously, in my class I frequently talk about a host of very real dilemmas that my students are inevitably going to face (if they have not yet already), such as drugs, gangs, dropping out, and sex. It not only makes for lively conversations but also helps students understand the very real potholes and dangers that lurk out there for them. My focus when I speak about these things is not to moralize or lecture, but just to get kids to recognize that they have choices and that the choices they make in regard to these matters are going to carry a lot of weight in determining their futures. Choice and consequence, intelligent decision making, thought before action, that sort of thing. Typical teacher stuff, right?

One day, Maria stuck around after class and asked to speak to me one-on-one.

"Sure," I said. "What's up?"

She looked troubled.

"Well," Maria began, "I wanted to know if I could address your AVID class tomorrow."

"Uh . . . Okay, sure. May I ask why?"

"Because . . . ," she paused. I could see that Maria was about to hit me with something huge. "Because, you know how you were talking to the girls about self-esteem and not just going along with a guy because of the pressure and stuff? 'Cause, you know, a girl could get pregnant?"

"Yeah," I said.

"Mr. Alan, I have a baby."

"Oh my goodness," I thought. Though I had known this student for almost three years, I'd had no idea.

Maria went on to tell me that during her sophomore year of high school, she lost her virginity one night in a park to a senior who pressured her into having sex—and then, basically, she never heard from him again. The reason she wasn't around much during her junior year was that she was occupied with being pregnant and giving birth. However, through a Home Studies program, Maria had earned enough credits to stay academically eligible, and she had returned for her senior year of high school. Her plan was to graduate, go to nursing school, and become a registered nurse.

I then learned that during the school day, Maria's mother stayed home and watched the baby while Maria went to class. And with all the baby stuff going on in my own life (my wife was pregnant at the time with our first), I must have spent months ominously warning my teens that while having a kid was the greatest thing ever to happen to me, waiting to have kids of their own until it was a time in their lives when they had first taken care of finishing their education, creating a solid foundation in their lives, building a support system around them, and so on was Vital with a capital V.

If ever there was a time I felt like the worst teacher on the planet, it was during my conversation with Maria. "How could I be such an insensitive, thoughtless moron to be rambling on about the folly of teenage pregnancy in front of a girl who just recently became the exact representation of everything about which I was prophesizing as doomsday?" Here I was playing up the foolishness, the dangers, the fact that many guys end up bailing out on the girls, leaving them to deal with the baby themselves—all in front of a girl who was living out the exact scenario I had been describing.

"Real smooth, Alan," I thought to myself. "Real smooth."

Why did I always have to push it with my kids? Couldn't I just teach the difference between similes and metaphors like everybody else? See, that's the flip side of being a teacher who goes beyond the scope of the prescribed curriculum with students in order to build relationships and keep classes relevant to the lives of teens; when you make mistakes, they are often big and bold.

"Of course you can speak to the class," I said. The next day, Maria went on to give one of the bravest speeches I have ever seen a student give.

"Hey, you guys. Remember how yesterday Mr. Alan was talking about being careful 'cause you could end up pregnant? Well . . . I have a baby."

The class got so quiet that the only sound that could be heard was the soft hum of my computer in the background.

Maria went on to tell the other kids about the challenges, about being ostracized by both her family and other students, about how she, of course, loved her baby but while other seniors were talking about affording prom tickets, she was thinking about affording diapers. Maria had no social life. For her, school was a way to avoid the second-biggest mistake that many teenage mothers make. First they get pregnant, and then they drop out. Well, Maria got pregnant but she understood the value of education and knew that fighting for her schooling now, no matter how tough it got, would put both her and her baby in a better situation later in life.

I cried. It was the bravest talk I'd ever heard a teenager give.

I was also proud. And sad. And angry, especially at the father who ran away. I even yelled at all my boys in the class, telling them that if they ever found themselves in that situation, at minimum it was their absolute responsibility to step up and not run away because it takes two to tango. The boys in my class stared back with fearful looks on their faces while I ripped into them about the responsibility of being a man.

"But we didn't even do anything, Mr. Alan," one of them finally said.

"Yeah . . . well . . . you better not," I warned.

Maria laid out her plans to graduate and then enroll in nursing school. Of course, at that moment she had become a role model to my other students in a way that I had never envisioned.

And she became a role model to me as well. I admired her, I rooted for her, and I took great inspiration from the quality of her character as she opened up and shared with my AVID class all the challenging details of her life as a single mother. The truth is it's kids like Maria who make teachers like me never want to leave the classroom.

This feeling I have about working with teenagers in a wi-fi, hip-hop where-has-all-the-sanity-gone world is the motivating force that drives me to teach from my heart as well as from my mind because the fact of the matter is I just never know whom I am going to reach, when I am going to reach them, or how I am going to reach them—even if it's just by standing aside so that someone else can do the teaching for a while.

The fact is, I am always on display. I am always being scrutinized, I am always being watched, and I am always sending messages as to how a person should behave, act, or react even when I have no intention of doing so. Why? Because, as I've learned, teenagers are always paying attention. They're always listening. They always have their little antennae up, even when they don't appear to be doing so.

Sure, they may tune out mundane things like the evening's homework. (There are times in my class when I have written assignments on the board in 4-foot-tall lettering and still had kids come to me the next day, look me straight in the eye, and tell me without a hint of guile, "Sorry, I just never saw it.") However, should I be curt, insensitive, intolerant, abrupt, unfair, or abrasive to a student, even if it's in hushed tones, it instantly registers with not only the individual student with whom I am speaking but every other kid in my class, even the ones who are 50 feet away.

And then it gets relayed to every other student I teach during lunchtime, after school, or on MySpace.

"That Mr. Alan, what a jerk. Did you hear what he did to . . . ?"

All my behavior, I realize, either contributes to or detracts from my ability to effectively teach and reach my students. There is simply no way around it because teens don't learn well from people they don't respect, but they do open up their ears and their brains to people they hold in high regard. Therefore, how I carry and conduct myself matters. It matters tremendously. And it matters all the time.

For example, a student of mine named Edna once asked me if she could get her book from a friend to whom she had lent it, so I gave her a pass, told her to go ahead, and moved on to deal with the 73 other things I was juggling at the moment. Five minutes later a fellow teacher blustered into my room with Edna in tow, tears in Edna's eyes, shouting at me, "You know, there are other people at this damn school who are trying to teach, too!" Literally, he was shouting at me, reading me the riot act in front of 36 of my own kids.

And Edna, of course, was one of those mild-mannered, sweet little students who had almost never done anything inappropriate—not even chew gum in class—so I knew it wasn't as if she had impolitely disrupted his class.

I just stood there. And listened. I listened as my colleague accused me of thinking I was the only teacher on campus who actually tried to get any work done, I listened as he told me that he was going to have Edna suspended for three days from school for illegally interrupting his class, and I listened as he told me that I had a hell of a nerve to think that the needs of "Mr. Author's class" were greater than the needs of "li'l ol' his."

He shouted, he barked, and he raged like an angry bull.

And then, when he was done blasting me, every student in my class turned to stare at me, waiting for my response.

So I apologized. Humbly. I told this teacher that, yes, I had written Edna a pass and, yes, I hadn't given much thought as to the impact it would have on his class, and, yes, in hindsight, I had to admit I was pretty thoughtless about the way in which the situation went down.

No excuses. No counterarguments with any shouting of my own. No pointing out the inappropriateness of his own behavior toward me.

None of that. And why? Because, as I tell my students all the time, when it comes to our actions, we always have a choice. We can choose to respond to other people with anger and hostility or we can choose not to. And here was my chance to prove it, an opportunity to teach something to my students I'd often preached.

See, unfortunately, violence and fights—between both boys and girls—are a very frequent occurrence on our campus, and I've spent countless hours discouraging my kids from getting entangled in altercations that can lead to suspension from school, incurring the wrath of other kids' homies so that they suddenly have enemies in the halls, and things like that. Nothing good ever comes out of violence on our campus, I tell my kids.

Ever.

Therefore, what I tell my students is, "Don't engage. Show some poise. Be smart, be disciplined, and walk away before matters escalate." It's been my advice for about a thousand teaching years. Keep focused on your long-term goals and the potential consequences of your actions.

I am convinced that if only more teens would learn to walk away when someone was "actin' the fool," a great many violent confrontations in our schools, as well as on our nation's streets, could be avoided.

See, our job is not one that exists solely within the confines of developing academic skills. Our job encompasses teaching a whole host of character traits that exist in addition to the hard skills of classroom subject areas. And teaching these matters of character is a responsibility to our students that simply can't be shirked. The fallacy that a person gets hired solely to teach academic material and does not have to embrace the responsibility of being a fair, tolerant, moral, and just role model in the classroom and around the campus is a responsibility that I, as a teacher, have no right to think I can absolve myself from. It goes with the territory, whether we like it or not.

This is where my fellow teachers at Lynwood High really shine. They embrace the idea that they are role models and go out of their way in a myriad of different ways (ways that rarely get much fanfare, mind you) to set a positive example for our students because they know a great many of our kids lack strong role models in their lives outside of class.

For example, once a few years ago I saw one of Lynwood High's Hispanic teachers spend hundreds of dollars out of his own pocket to barbecue carne asada so that the Latino parents in our community would feel appreciated for making the effort to visit the classrooms where their kids went to school. (Of course everyone got to eat, though.) He knew that many of the parents were taking time off work—off nonsalaried work, meaning their household incomes were suffering so that they could attend the event—to help support their children's learning, and he wanted to reach out to them in a manner that would leave them with a good impression of our school while simultaneously expressing our hope for their continued support. As I watched the tremendously positive reception to his barbecue unfold, I realized that his was an idea that never even crossed my mind, yet not only did it cross his but he acted on it at his own great expense.

Then, when I gave him big props for doing what he had done, he told me something quite insightful. He said, "Kids need to see themselves as part of the community and it's my job to show that to them." Of course, the kids he was referring to were the ones running the barbecue, the students with tattoos, low grades, and a history of being troublemakers. Yet, here they were, being of service to everyone who walked through the front gate of our school. Instead of treating these kids like they were the enemy of the community, he treated them as if they were the fabric of the community, and they responded in kind with smiles, respect, and a ton of self-esteem on display for all to see.

"Teaching kids to serve and help one another is important," this teacher told me. "It's a big part of my culture."

"Me, I never think about serving white people," I answered. "Heck, it almost sounds racist for me to even entertain the idea," I added with a guilty laugh.

"Brown-skin people try to take care of their own," he told me as he passed me a warm tortilla filled with freshly grilled meats. I walked back to my room with feelings of admiration. Sure, some white people are exceptionally generous, but there is definitely not a cultural mandate to be kind to those of the same background like I've witnessed in the Latino community. It's commendable. Highly commendable. Matter of fact, if there is one thing my students, the staff, and the community of Lynwood have often shown me, it's that people who have less are often more generous than those who have more.

Another year I had a very deep, very melancholic "What's it all about?" conversation with an African American teacher who was once a student at Lynwood High himself. Now, while most folks who go to Lynwood dream of attending college one day so they can get out of the hood, he told me he went to college in order to one day return to the hood in order to make it a better place.

Talk about a hometown hero—wow. And he's not alone. Lynwood High School has a lot of teachers on staff who were once students who returned to teach at our school for this very same reason. Truly, I am always deeply impressed by the character of these folks. They're the staff members who do all the extracurricular stuff, the ones who stay late for prom, come early for pep rallies, chaperone dances, sacrifice weekends, and on and on to offer our students more than just a between-the-bells teacher effort. Truly, they are some of the finest role models on our campus.

We must always remember that teens are paying attention, teens are acutely perceptive, and teens are fantastically attuned to the humanity of the educator as well as the unspoken messages teachers send. Therefore, if I want my students to be respectful to me, to one another, or to the rules of our classroom, I must first be respectful of them. If I want my students to come to class prepared to learn, I must first come to class prepared to teach. If I want my students to do anything at all, the very first rule I must not violate is *avoid hypocrisy at all costs.*

Do what I say and not what I do is the absolute worst teaching strategy there is.

Yes, the students are always paying attention. Even when it seems they're not. This is why I am such a strong believer in assuming ownership for our actions and then teaching this skill to teens.

Classrooms are, after all, living, breathing spaces, and teachers are living, breathing examples of all the insights, wisdom, and knowledge that we seek to impart. We don't have to be perfect—we are most certainly allowed to be fallible humans and make mistakes—but in no unquestionable terms, the teachers' reach should always exceed their grasp.

Teach Teens to Take Ownership

I love my kids, but goodness gracious, there are times when my students drive me crazy. Crazy!

I mean, there's almost a sense of learned, give-no-real-and-true-effort mentality embedded into the culture of teens in urban Title I schools that is absolutely maddening for those of us who work here. The mentality is so poisonous it might possibly be the single biggest reason so many inner-city schools such as mine underperform to the large degree that we do. And it all boils down to effort; teens at urban schools all across America are simply giving much less effort toward the accomplishment of their academic goals, tasks, and assignments than the teens who attend wealthy suburban schools.

And like I said, it drives me crazy.

(By the way, this is not racist—and if you think it is, just google a small little topic known as "the achievement gap," and you'll find about a hundred million pieces of statistical data to back me up.)

Now, sure, I could blame parents. I could blame former teachers. I could blame school superintendents, the media, the president of the United States, and so forth, but I am of the opinion that better than pointing fingers is finding solutions to these incredibly vexing problems, so I've asked myself, "Why are my teens so keen to avoid taking ownership over their studies, their behavior, and even their lives?"

I've come to the conclusion that it centers on commitment.

Commitment, to resort to clichés for a moment, is a willingness to lay it on the line, to give it your all, to reach down deep and with no holds barred, let the best that you have to offer fly. Unfortunately, lay-it-on-the-line commitment is a quality far too rarely seen in far too many teenagers

> Low skills are not the problem; low skill levels are the by-product of the problem. The real issue is that teaching teens . . . requires motivating students to commit to their own education. They need to be vested. The more fully so, the higher their performance.

in today's wi-fi, hip-hop world.

Oddly enough, teaching actual academic skills is one of the easiest parts of my classroom job. Truly, I can't remember the last time that my students' low levels of ability were the foremost impediment to me reaching my kids. And being that I, as previously mentioned, regularly have kids in high school that read and write years below grade level, this claim is no small statement. Look, if tenth graders have fourth-grade reading abilities, we'll start there. And if they have eighth-grade writing skills, we'll begin there. And if they have twelfth-grade literacy skills, we'll take it from there. Truly, the only way to be an effective teacher is to start where the kids' abilities are and then work diligently toward advancing them.

However, as I said, the low skill levels of my students are not the real obstacle for me, and I do get them to work through some very sophisticated literature, as evidenced by the fact that I successfully teach those very same aforementioned low-skill students such works as the entire, unabridged text of William Shakespeare's *Hamlet*. And they get it.

And they like it. (Well, it appears they like it, but they most assuredly get it.)

No, low skills are not the problem; low skill levels are the by-product of the problem. The real issue is that teaching teens and reaping results in a wi-fi, hip-hop, where-has-all-the-sanity-gone world requires motivating students to commit to their own education.

They need to be vested. The more fully so, the higher their performance.

Look, I can teach how to properly identify gerund phrases to practically any teen—any teen who really wants to learn it, that is. But the kids who tune out, refuse to come to class, won't do their homework, or give me a lick of effort toward their studies are kids whom I am going to have just as much difficulty reaching as any other teacher in America. There are thousands of books out there that address how to teach skills in each and every classroom subject area, but none of them will do a bit of good if the teacher cannot get the students to take ownership over their own learning and try.

Yep, they need to try. It's an element of our national schooling dialogue that we pay virtually no official attention to on a formal level, yet it's key to helping us reap the results we seek to obtain in our nation's classrooms.

Study any successful inner-city charter school in a dilapidated community that is delivering uncharacteristically high test scores and you will see that the core ingredient of their secret sauce is that their students are actually trying to do well.

Conversely, examine the effort being put forth by the students at a so-called failing school in a similarly disadvantaged environment and you'll discover that a heck of a lot of kids are simply not really trying. Their effort stinks.

Remember, when teens take ownership for their actions and behavior and authentically dedicate themselves to their work, good things happen.

Tips for Teaching Teens to Take Ownership

Know the Role That Fear Plays

Good ol'-fashioned fear is driving the bus for way too many teenagers. However, I kind of get that. I mean, for teens to really give their all means that they will be on display in some way, and if adolescence is anything, it's a period in life very much characterized by tremendous insecurity. Therefore, when we ask kids to really try, what we're truly asking them to do is to be vulnerable and open up. But teenagers don't like to feel vulnerable—they already feel vulnerable enough—so their own internal defense mechanisms tell them not to risk the potential shame, humiliation, and overexposure that trying their hardest, testing their limits, and genuinely committing to a task might incur. Coming up short always stings, but never more so than when you've tried your hardest. Not giving their best effort, on the other hand, leaves teens an escape hatch to not feel like crud for coming up short because they can always tell themselves, "Well, yeah, but that's because I didn't really try in the first place." It's a circular, dysfunctional, self-fulfilling logic driven, at its core, by simple fear.

Providing an emotionally safe environment for teens to open themselves up will result in greater commitment, effort, and energy toward accomplishing classroom—and life—tasks.

Make Sure Teens Have the Skill Levels to Be Successful

I once heard the United States secretary of education make a comment about making sure that "no child was left behind" in reference to English language learners, and she was insisting that testing was a solid means of ensuring language learners were getting the education they needed. But I thought to myself, "You know, if we sent you, Ms. Secretary of Education, to Albania for two years and then expected you to solve mathematical word problems and identify the usage of figurative language in tests that were exclusively written in Albanian, chances are you probably wouldn't do too well. Two years is simply not enough time to hold such high expectations for language fluency." And if we pounded her with tests for long and hard enough, our secretary of education would most probably get frustrated and angry and start to feel a lowered sense of self-worth (or anger at the folks who kept testing her on things she couldn't reasonably be expected to yet know). The basic concept is not too hard: if a person does not have the skills needed to be successful, that person can't be expected to perform. Here's a quick test.

Take a look at two problems I made up, based on the format of our school's mandated standardized tests, and really try to solve them. And keep in mind that these are two questions designed to evaluate the *mathematical* ability of my students.

1. Two consecutive positive integers have the property that one integer times twice the other equals 612. What is the sum of these two integers?

   a. 33

   b. 35

   c. 37

   d. 39

2. Beth is two years older than Julio. Gerald is twice as old as Beth. Debra is twice as old as Gerald. The sum of their ages is 38. How old is Beth?

a. 3

b. 5

c. 6

d. 8

Though it makes me want to laugh when I read these problems, this is not a joke. As anyone can clearly see, before these are math problems, they are reading comprehension problems, and I would venture to say that most people who read these two questions quickly give up on trying to solve them. Why?

Because when people do not believe they can be successful, they won't even try to do the work. And really, who knows better than teens when they have been set up to fail? It's only when teenagers have the sense that they can do the task being asked of them that they will give a full and genuine effort. Make sure teens have the skills to perform that which is being required of them—or have tools to learn the skills—before placing any demands. Otherwise, teens will tune out.

(By the way, I wonder how our secretary of education would do on the two sample problems . . . in Albanian or not. Maybe now people can see why being labeled as a so-called failing school is so frustrating to so many of us—the assessments are, in my opinion, phenomenally unreasonable.)

🔵 Watch for the Three Enemies of Taking Ownership

Trying to Put Lipstick on a Pig

When I was 40, I had my very first proctological exam. No matter how important it might have been for my health, the truth is I dreaded the idea from the moment I was informed of this midlife rite of medical passage and I sought to put the doctor's visit off for months. Matter of fact, the only thing about that day I recall with anything other than dismay was when my physician, sensing my uneasiness, told me that if it was any consolation, the experience wasn't going to be the highlight of his day either. Very funny, right? Well, when it comes to teens, great dislike of the process can very often be an insurmountable hurdle, especially in school. If kids hate the work, they very often won't do it, and no matter how you try to sell it to them, sometimes they just don't want any part of certain activities. Recognize this and adjust accordingly. Trying to put lipstick on a pig—pretending something is all rosy when it most clearly is not—will only result in your losing credibility with teens. Be honest. Be forthright. Speak to the problems, the challenges, and the unpleasant aspects instead of pretending these elements don't exist. And if it's obvious from the get-go they are not going to like the process, see if there are other options, but if there aren't, tell them so. Just don't pretend that teens are going to love what they are being asked to do when both you and they know it's going to be a task they'll not particularly enjoy.

Not Crafting a Specific, Singular Moment of Pact

Without a real dedication, a vow, a singular moment of declaration that a teen will pursue an objective and see it through to the end, the chances for a teenager to take full ownership are greatly diminished. Know the strength in making a declaration, whether on paper, via a handshake, or through an oral agreement. But have a moment of truth, a "Once you sign this, you are committing" type of experience that, once complete, is like the beginning of a journey from which the kids can never go back. As a teacher I know the immense value of utilizing these types of tools—but only after first getting teens to participate in the construction of the agreements. Allowing teens to set their own expectations is much better than telling them what their expectations should be. As I've discovered, teens always take more ownership when they feel involved as participants in the construction of agreements.

In my own class, this starts with the class rules at the beginning of the year. Instead of me simply handing out a sheet of my rules, I take a few moments and have my students brainstorm a list of rules that they think we, as a class, need to follow in order to have a productive year. Of course, they try to sneak some goofy ones into the final version, like "No homework on days of the week that have the letter y in them," but experience proves to me that if I allow my students to feel as if they've crafted their own rules, they find the enforcement of the rules much more reasonable.

And once our rules are set, we make a pact to abide by them, a moment of demarcation that, from this point on, these are our classroom guidelines. (I, of course, have veto power and the right to add rules whenever I wish; democracy is not the system of government in my classroom.)

Discounting the Importance of the Embarrassment Factor

Taking ownership over something means standing for something, and teens who are bold enough to make such a claim in their lives open themselves up to the slings and arrows of other kids. And, as we all know, kids can be downright mean to one another. For teens, it's much easier to remain noncommittal because then there is less chance of being picked on or teased. However, embarrassment should not be what teenagers are afraid of when it comes to doing their work in areas of their lives such as school. Flunking out, having a limited ability to earn a solid income, feeling forced to turn to a life of crime, drugs, jail, and low self-esteem . . . now that's what they should be afraid of. But getting up in front of the class to try to explain what they know about Charles Dickens?

Public speaking should not be the biggest monster in their bedroom closet.

Where embarrassment reigns, logic often flees, and while not giving their all may cost kids on the external front in terms of grades, goals, and achievements, it saves them on the personal front in terms of potential shame, humiliation, and embarrassment. Of course it doesn't make sense, but hey, teenage emotions rarely do.

Remember, the dread of embarrassment frequently—and unnecessarily—impedes teens from taking ownership.

8

Because You Just Never Know
Teaching Teens to Seek Excellence

I was named the state of California's 2007 Teacher of the Year. It turned out to be the most magical, exciting, and humbling experience of my professional life. I had the privilege to meet thousands of educators; see schools across the country through a local, state, and federal perspective; and chat with people at every rung on the ladder of classroom life. I met the chief executive officers of huge educational corporations, teachers at all grade levels, and kids in every possible school situation, from teens sweating their Ivy League college applications to juveniles in jail facing years behind bars who were mandated by the courts to continue their "education" but weren't even allowed access to hardcover books because they could be far too easily fashioned into weapons.

Talk about seeing the spectrum of education in this country—*wow.* I even met the president of the United States in the Oval Office. Like I said, the experience was just incredible.

It was also the most amount of work I've ever done in my entire life.

Since California, unlike many other of our nation's states, does not give its Teacher of the Year a sabbatical to go along with the honor and obligations of the award, I pretty much found myself bouncing right back into my classroom to teach things like dissecting symbolism in a poetic text after arriving home on a late-night flight from goodness knows where after giving a Teacher of the Year speech at a school, business, organization, or club the day before. Pretty soon, I became exhausted. Wiped out. I became physically, mentally, and emotionally drained like never before.

In part it was because I felt almost manically driven to try to use whatever platform I had from winning Teacher of the Year to create positive change in educational areas that, in my opinion, desperately needed help. To be honest, some people from other states became Teachers of the Year and treated the award as more of a ceremonial honor, waving like Rose Bowl Parade queens, smiling for the cameras, and saying all the right, polite things in interviews with the press. But I realized early on that I felt personally compelled to try to do something meaningful with the honor in an attempt to improve the state of public education. I held discussions with members of Congress, I spoke at school assemblies, and I reached out to other educators and teenagers across the nation to offer whatever materials, insights, or assistance I could give. And as I clearly (and unfortunately) saw, thousands of our nation's teachers felt starved for tools that would authentically reach their own students. Therefore, in an effort to bring some of the effective materials and lesson plans I used in my own classroom to teachers and teens everywhere, I built a website filled with pages and pages of free resources.

The site contains essay prep for the SAT exam, complimentary study guides to the young adult novels I have written, sample lessons on how to use hip-hop in the classroom, interviews with a host of dynamic people throughout the world of education and young adult literature, and useful links to a multitude of other websites so that teachers and teens can find the resources they need to be more productive in their own classrooms and lives. Essentially, I created a large collection of resources that were free of charge so that students like mine in schools across the country could have a bank of no-fee, well-crafted materials available to them to assist them on their journey to becoming well educated. My website's motto became "Just click, print, and go." (For more information, please visit www.alansitomer.com.)

Being of service to the teachers and teens of this state and nation in whatever fashion I could became of paramount importance to me, yet clearly I was burning the candles at both ends. And with a new baby at home (as I said, my first, a girl named Sienna, to whom I have dedicated this book), my professional obligations relentlessly growing, and virtually no days off in any given month to recharge my batteries, I became so overworked I ran out of gas.

Entirely.

"Hey, Mr. Alan," a student said to me one day when she walked into my room. "You look like crap."

That's what I love about teenagers. They'll tell you straight up how it is. But this student didn't mean it in a bad way; she said it with affection, with concern in her voice. And the truth is I probably did look like crap. After all, a person can only take so much.

"Your problem is," a friend told me that weekend when I relayed the story to him, "you need to learn to say no. People are asking you to do stuff almost all of the time nowadays and you never turn them down."

It was true, I said to myself. I worked very hard at being accommodating. It went with the role of being California's Teacher of the Year, I thought.

"You gotta say no to some stuff, man. You're killing yourself," my friend told me. "And guess what . . . you're allowed. You are allowed to turn some things down."

It was a real insight for me. It never dawned on me that saying no to certain requests was an option.

Well, guess what happened two days later when I got a phone call from this guy named Bill to accept a special recognition from a certain chamber of commerce? That's right; I said no.

"Thanks, but no thanks," I told him politely.

Saying no felt good. "Wow," I thought to myself. "I really can do this." But the next day Bill called me again.

"Look, I appreciate the thought, I really do, but I am so run-down right now that I am trying to pull back on my engagements. Really, thanks, but no thanks, Bill," I said and then I ended the call. Politely, of course.

But Bill persisted. He called me once. He called me twice. He called me a third time. He even had the nerve to call me directly in my classroom on my school phone while I was teaching, right smack in the middle of second period.

"Look Bill, I can't talk right now."

"But I'd really like you to reconsider because. . . ."

"Bill . . . I can't talk. I'm in the middle of class."

"Alan," he said to me. "You don't understand, it would mean so much to. . . ."

"Look, Bill, I cannot talk right now," I reemphasized. And then I made the number one mistake you are never supposed to make when someone is hounding and hounding you.

I gave Bill my cell phone number.

For the next 17,000 days in a row, I got a call from Bill. I got calls from Bill at 7 A.M and I got calls from Bill at 9 P.M. I got call after call after call from Bill. Finally, his persistence and optimistic nature wore me down.

"Okay, I'll do it," I finally said. "Just tell me where and when."

With a smile in his voice, he gave me the information.

"But is there a chance this can go on early? I mean, I'd really like to make it home to see my daughter before she goes to bed," I asked him.

This last part was quite important to me because I had grown to hate the days when I felt as though I was nothing more than a workaholic ghost in my own house. School started so early and Sienna was, bless her heart, such a great sleeper that quite often I was gone before she was up in the morning. And if I wasn't careful about my obligations, there would be times when I wouldn't return home until after she had gone to bed at night. Making it home early enough to put my daughter to sleep became a point on which I was not willing to compromise.

"It's a deal breaker, Bill. I'll do it, but you have to promise me that I'll make it home on time."

"You got it," he said, and we hung up.

It wasn't long before I regretted agreeing to show up for the event. As a matter of fact, for the entire week leading up to it, I was inventing creative ways to bail out.

I have a cough. "No, you need something better," I thought. *My daughter has a cough.* "No, better than that." *My pet turtle has a cough . . . and I'm scared he's gonna sneeze himself clear out of his shell. Really, I'd love to make it but. . . .*

For better or for worse, being a professional to me means honoring my word, so I didn't make up any kind of hokey story and I did what I said I would do. I showed up.

Five minutes after arriving I discovered the event was going to start about an hour and fifteen minutes later than the time I had been told it would begin. Ooh, I was mad.

Plus, I had an extra hour and fifteen minutes to stew, time enough to sit in my car, pretend to read a book, and evolve from general agitation to outright bitterness.

Finally, when I went up to the front offices of the city hall, I was greeted by a group of people I'd never met before.

"Excuse me, has anybody seen Bill?"

Bill, apparently, hadn't arrived yet. However, once I was identified as California's Teacher of the Year, lots of folks wanted to start having their pictures taken with me. Seems there was an upcoming local election of some sort.

Most people were friendly about it, but some folks seemed like they had ulterior motives, like the gentleman who wore a shiny three-piece, grey-and-purple suit with a watch chain, tie pin, gold necklace, three bracelets, diamond-crusted wristwatch, and ring on every finger. Plus, he had Jheri curls in his hair (I didn't even know they still had Jheri curls.)

"Yo teacher man, lemme snap a photo with ya."

"Uhm . . . have you seen Bill?" I asked.

"Yeah sure, right over here. Me and the best teacher in the nation o' California."

He pulled me close and smiled wide. Goodness knows what my face was about to be used to endorse. Meanwhile, I kept asking, "Where's Bill?"

"Not here yet."

Picture. Smile. Snap.

"Anybody seen Bill?"

Picture. Smile. Snap.

"Nope, not here yet."

"Excuse me," I asked, growing more and more aggravated. "Can somebody please tell me where I can find Bill?"

"Oh, he's around the corner," someone finally informed me.

I hoisted my belt and stormed for the corner, ready to give Bill a piece of my mind. The event was running late, I was going to miss my daughter's bedtime, and I had just endorsed Mr. Superfly for deputy mayor. Plus, I was flat-out wrecked from being overworked like I'd never before been in my entire life and I just wanted to go home, deal with the inevitable 378 e-mails I'd have on my computer, and get some rest.

With all of these negative emotions swirling through my brain, I turned the corner and saw Bill.

Sitting in a wheelchair. Bill, it turns out, was a quadriplegic.

"Alan," he said with a warm smile. "Come gimme a hug, man. I can't tell you what an inspiration your work has been to my life. Really, thank you so much for making it today."

My heart sank. Oh my goodness, I . . . I had no idea.

> **What life was clearly showing me, I realized, was that the whole role of being a teacher was never about the teacher; it was about all the people that teachers endeavored to positively affect.**

"Uh, yeah," I stammered. "Of course."

I leaned in to hug a man I'd never before met, a man who, from his wheelchair, was greeting me as if I was one of the reasons he'd found in this world to continue forging on in life. And there was only one thing I could think.

"Could I be any more of a self-absorbed ass?"

I went on to listen as Bill explained how hard he had worked to convince the city council that it needed to honor me because of all the good work I was doing with the community's kids. Gangs had stolen far too many of our students from their families, and having a Teacher of the Year who also wrote young adult novels for Disney . . . well, that needed to be recognized, he said.

I sat there completely floored, my heart having turned to jelly. All the bitterness, all the anger, all the frustration, exhaustion, and discontent disappeared immediately. Instead, I felt instantaneously grateful.

Grateful for my health.

Grateful for my family.

Grateful for my career being something that provided me with a means of reaching out to so many people, more people than I ever even realized I had touched.

"What a fool you are, Alan." That's all I could think of. What life was clearly showing me, I realized, was that the whole role of being a teacher was never about the teacher; it was about all the people that teachers endeavored to positively affect.

It was at this moment of my career that I was reminded why I must always strive to give my best. Because as a teacher, you just never know whom you are going to reach.

Seek Excellence

Let's be clear about one thing: I love our schools! Absolutely love 'em! Even the hard-to-love ones.

I love the kids, I love the subject matter, I love the books, I love the energy, I love the look of the weird meats being served at lunchtime, and I love the freaky way that when it's time for me to take summer vacation, I long for having another few weeks of class just so I can do a smidgen more work with my students before I set the little birdies free to fly away, most of them on their way to leaving my rectangular little educational nest forever.

My love for my profession stems from my insider's view of schools as places that offer hope, resources, counseling, accommodations for those with special needs, sports, music, theater, dance, career guidance, technology, encouragement, books, community meeting sites, art, water fountains, libraries, restrooms, differentiated instruction, and even pencils at absolutely no charge whatsoever to kids all across the country regardless of where they come from or what they have to offer in return. In my estimation, our nation's schools are phenomenally commendable institutions if for no other reason than the spirit of giving and serving they embody. When you boil it down, our schools have been designed for the sole purpose of benefiting kids. That's pretty noble stuff, and like most educators, I feel incredibly proud of my chosen career.

Without a doubt, teaching makes a person feel good.

So why are schools such a magnet for virtually relentless criticism from every flank of society? (And hey, I knock 'em, too. Matter of fact, I knock them a lot. Yet why?)

After much deliberation I've come to realize that for me, it's because I want excellence. Not okay-ness. Not mediocrity. Not kind-of-all-right-ness. Excellence!

Excellence is, rightly so, the bedrock of all my expectations when it comes to schooling.

No wonder I'm always so ready to blast away . . . I'm constantly disappointed!

Arrgh.

Unfortunately, though, it's my own fault, as I've set myself up for a classic lose-lose scenario. On one hand, I expect our classrooms to be supremely successful, yet on the other hand, I know they're underfunded, overcrowded, inefficient, poorly managed, and ill-equipped to handle the diverse needs society is requiring them to manage. Though our schools are not being given the tools to do what I demand they do, I still expect them to meet the standards I mandate. Really, if anything, it's my preposterously

> **I must always encourage my students to search for and embrace their own inner excellence, no matter what the circumstances on the outside are, because the fact is, as a teacher, you just never know when your relentless drive toward expecting excellence from your students will make all the difference in the world to them.**

high expectations that are the problem here.

My ideals are over-the-top.

And by holding onto them the way I do, I am perpetually setting myself up for *immense* disappointment. However, what the heck am I supposed to do?

Should I lower my aims? Should I seek less from the kids at Lynwood High? Should we as a nation lower the bar for what we expect our schools to be able to deliver to the next generation of young adults in terms of their education, aspirations, or preparedness for the future?

Of course not! Teens today already have their backs up against the wall in so many ways that not to hold the highest of expectations for them, or for our schools, is inexcusable. The point is nonnegotiable.

If there is one thing I've learned as a teacher, it's that I absolutely must always encourage my students to search for and embrace their own inner excellence, no matter what the circumstances on the outside are, because the fact is, as a teacher, you just never know when your relentless drive toward expecting excellence from your students will make all the difference in the world to them.

As a teacher, I've learned you just never know when you're going to get through.

CL wrote the following letter to me (I was her teacher for three years) after being accepted to her top choice of colleges, San Jose State University, a school far away from her past life in the city of Los Angeles. After she earns her degree, CL hopes to become a law enforcement agent.

A Letter to Mr. Alan

Many people really do not know where I am from, or where I come from. I can hide my feelings so well that people will not have any idea of everything I have been through. I come from a world of violence, drugs and gangs. Many people say I act and look like a normal girl. I have an appearance of a good girl but guess what I am not. When I first started at Lynwood High I did not care about anything. I never took time to think about the future or even think about where I was going to end up in the future. All that was going through my mind was my friends, my boyfriend and being on the streets. All I wanted to do was get high and act a fool. It was rare when I would go to school; I did not like it and had no interest in it what so ever. I would call up my friends and tell them that I was not going to school and that was it. I would leave and not come back til after twelve at night. I have done some bad things. Things that nobody but my friends and God know about. I really do regret what I have done in the past and I regret hurting all the people have. If I can change what I have done in the past I would. I would change everything. Their has been times where I have been woken up in the middle of the night where I had to get up and go out to the streets and take care of business. I had to go out and get money on my own; I would sell drugs. I always had to have my friends back when they needed me if not then it was me on the line. I never imagined that hanging around with the people that I did was going to turn me into a person that I did not want to be. In the ninth grade that's when everything fell apart. I got involved with the wrong crowd and that was when I first got initiated into my first gang. It was the worst feeling ever and I wished I'd never did it and would go back. As I sit here and write this

(continued on next page)

paper I think about how stupid I was and how I never want to go back to my old ways. I realized that the most when I saw my best friend get shot in her head and I watched as her head swelled up. As soon as I got over her loss that's when I said to myself that I did not want to live that life any more. I did not want to be the next person to die. So I made up my mind that I was not going back. I was scared at first but I had to do what I had to do. I told my friends that I did not want to be involved any more. They told me to think long and hard about what I was saying and so I did. I was scared knowing that if I went outside people were going to come after me. I was scared to go out of my house knowing that something could happen to me at any time of day. But I had to get out. I did not want to keep making the wrong choices. I started coming to school. Mr. Alan was a big part of this change. He taught me to learn that no matter what happens you can always get back up and try again. I did not let anything stop me from getting my education. Mr. Alan was the one who taught me to be proactive. I admit at first I would just sit in class and space out not really caring what he had to say but later it would get to me. I started really thinking about things he said and about turning my life around and so I did. I started hanging out with different people and got my things together. I had never thought about graduating because I thought I would always be a low life but Mr. Alan told me I had a chance to be something in life and now I do whatever I can not to lose that opportunity. It makes me so proud to know that I have now accomplished something in life by getting into college. Now that I have this, I won't let anyone take it away from me.

Signed,

CL

As teachers, we must realize that we are role models, parents, mentors, friends, confessors, confidants, stand-up comedians, fans, instructors, bearers of bad news, bedrocks of inspiration, frail little human beings, coaches, pillars of strength, voices of authority, and a thousand other things all day long, with no rhyme or reason to the pattern by which we will be called to do any of these duties.

And often we're asked to do them with no prior notice or training while simultaneously performing multiple other jobs at the same time.

Sometimes we do good . . .

Dear Mr. Alan,

Not too long ago we had a conversation in your class about how difficult it is to look back at our age and be able to appreciate things. Fortunately, I feel that for the most part I am able to see things for what they are worth as they are presented to me. Today is the last official day of my education here at Lynwood High School and though I am saddened by the things that must be left behind I am also glad to be moving onward to bigger and better things, but I am also grateful. Grateful to the people who I consider to be fundamental pieces to the person I am today and the person I hope to become.

This is why I thank you Mr. Alan. For the past three years you have been one of the most influential people that I have encountered and there are many things that I have learned from you that can't be found in a text book or a reading. I am unable to speak with anything but the utmost respect and admiration for you. I hope that you continue to be the excellent teacher that you are and that like you, many others may find themselves in places where they are most needed. Once again, thank you for everything Mr. Alan, you are a wonderful person and a great teacher

Sincerely,

Isaac

Ps. I hope we are able to keep in touch.

Sometimes we are befuddled . . .

I felt I just had 2 write 2 u about
a big issue that I'm having right now.
But u better keep it a secret cuz I don't
like anyone 2 know how I really feel.
Last of all no one really cares 1st
2nd I really don't like people 2 know,
only the ones that I feel are the
closest people in my life, and u a
big reason you're one of them. Anyways
what I wanted 2 get off my chest
is that I've been having a thought
in my mind about committing suicide. That's
why lately I haven't done any work,
I am depressed everywhere I go, and
I feel useless. I have had family problems
my whole life, and I want 2 stop the
suffering of my dad always bringing me
down in everything I do. One of these days
I'm gonna have 2 swing at his ass.
Then I had the weed problem, I feel so
regretful 4 that, that I want a new life. I really
don't know what 2 do, so I am asking
4 UR help!

Sometimes our hearts are torn apart . . .

Dear Colleagues and Students:

One of our tenth-grade student's father was shot and killed last Saturday. He was not involved in gangs, but was merely walking home from work and was shot as the shooters apparently aimed for others.

The family needs help to ship the body to Mexico and for burial.

I have the niece, a very nice twelfth-grade student, in my economics class. Needless to say, the family is devastated about the situation.

Many of my seniors have accepted the responsibility of helping this family, as they have been instructed about and participated in other community-based funding projects. Please assist my economics students in this worthy project.

Sincerely,
Social Studies Department

The donations will be picked up throughout today and Friday.

Sometimes we don't know on which side we should fight . . .

CANINES AND METAL DETECTORS

1. **CANINE SEARCH**

    Canine Search is a program established by the District which assists us in the process of finding controlled substances or people in possession of controlled substances while being on campus. As you have been informed before, the search is at random; therefore, there is no prior notification to the date and time of visiting classrooms or any office in relation to this matter. In fact, the school does not receive prior notification as to when the canine team is coming to our school. These processes ensure that not only classrooms and offices are searched at random but also the dates schools are visited is also done at random.

2. **METAL DETECTORS**

    The District has recommended the use of Metal Detectors on our campus

Sometimes our students accomplish things that make us smile ten miles wide.

Stanford University

Leland Stanford Junior University
announces that
Dontae Derrell Rayford
is a candidate for the degrees of
Bachelor of Arts
in
Sociology
and
Master of Arts
in
Sociology
at the One Hundred Sixteenth Commencement
Sunday, June seventeenth
Two Thousand Seven
at nine-thirty in the morning
Stanford Stadium
Stanford University

Sometimes our students face situations we can't quite comprehend . . .

> ABOUT A YEAR AGO MY DAD HAD TO SACRIFICE ALMOST TEN THOUSAND DOLLARS FOR MY UNCLE ADRIAN. THE SITUATION WAS THAT MY UNCLE WAS IMMIGRATING FROM NICARAGUA TO CALIFORNIA ILLEGALLY. THE PROBLEM WAS THAT AT FIRST IT WAS ONLY GOING TO BE FIVE THOUSAND FIVE HUNDRED DOLLARS BUT WHEN HE GOT HERE THEY WERE ASKING FOR A COUPLE OF MORE THOUSANDS, IT WAS LIKE THIS, YOU PAY THE MONEY AND HIS FREE TO GO, OR YOU DONT PAY THE MONEY HE DIES. AT THAT TIME WE DIDN'T HAVE A CHOICE, BUT FOR MY DAD TO PAY THE MONEY.

And sometimes we just want to hug our kids and let them know it's going to be okay:

My Mother Made Me

When I was four years old my father was arrested. He has been in jail ever since. My mother would always make me write him letters, send him birthday and father's day cards, and pictures of me. She told me he was still my father and that he missed me. I felt as if he failed me, so I never wanted to speak to him again. My mother didn't know what I was feeling, she couldn't possibly know. After all, she had a father when she grew up. I suffered much pain knowing, I would never see my father again. By me being so young, I didn't know how to express my feelings to myself or anyone else. In November, of last year, my mother made me stop writing to my father. I told her that I didn't want to waste my time writing to him. She could see how hurt I was, so she agreed that I didn't have to write to him unless I wanted to. As far as me gaining anything by writing him letters, I think not. I know I shouldn't hate him, but I do. I try to forgive him for the stupid mistakes he's made, but I can't. There's too much anger inside me. Hopefully, one day I will be able to forgive him.

The spectrum of emotions for educators who work with today's teenagers is surreal. Sometimes we laugh with a kid and feel terrible for him all at the same time:

> The grade I should get for this semester is an "F". One of the reason I should get an "F" is because I haven't done none of the work in the class. The second reason IS that I haven't been to school for like a month and a half. The last reason I should get a "F" is because I never pass the test or read the books.

Teaching teens means having your heart filled to the point of bursting by the smallest of notes from students you weren't even sure were paying attention:

> Honestly, I've never been in an english class where I had so much fun! Even though I didn't like the times when we would work on power paragraphs for a long time! But I loved when we would do individual/ Group projects. They taught to think outside the square! Thank you for everything.
>
> "Your the best teacher!"
> keep on the good work rn.
>
> Love ya!
>
> Take care
> never forget '06

It means having your faith shaken:

> *On Saturday, January 20, a Lynwood High School Alumni,*
> *Miguel, was shot and killed. His family and loved ones are*
> *collecting donations for his funeral expenses. If you would*
> *like to contribute to this fund, please come to the ASB window*
> *during first or second lunch to make your donation. Thank you*
> *for your prayers and condolences.*

Teaching means try as you might, there will be times when you just
don't know the right answer:

> Dear Mr. Sitomer,
>
> My name is Mona and I teach seventh and eighth grade
> English in Los Angeles County. I have been a huge fan of
> yours ever since I read THE HOOPSTER and HIP-HOP IN THE
> CLASSROOM.
>
> Congratulations on all of your well-earned awards!!
>
> I know that you already must have tons to do, but I am just
> curious to know your advice. How would you adjust your
> teaching strategies when you have as many as 42 students per
> period? (A period is 90 minutes each for our English classes.)
> Most students have never read an entire novel before and
> say that they are satisfied with a "D" grade. It seems hard to
> engage the students and we are required to use the textbook.
>
> I appreciate you taking the time to read this!
>
> Sincerely,
>
> Mona

And it means seeing the same issues and challenges surfacing in the lives of your students year after year after year.

Time Is of the Essence   *An essay by Amir*

My best friend Kevin was sent here to keep me on the straight and narrow path in life and in my opinion made the demolition sacrifice in order to teach me the essence of time and opportunity. Even though it is painful to relate the story at times, losing my best friend this past fall to a gang war inspired me to make the most of every opportunity because it may just be here for a short time.

Kevin and I were quite the dynamic duo before we were temporarily separated (as I like to think of it). I looked up to him because Kevin taught me a lot of things.

Teaching teens and reaping results in a wi-fi, hip-hop, where-has-all-the-sanity-gone world means that you need to have a compass by which you can navigate the demands of your own career and guide students as they deal with the host of unpredictable circumstances your kids will inevitably face. It's a simple fact of teaching in the modern age: you just never know when even the most minor of your day-by-day efforts will contribute in some small way to a spectacularly great development for one of your students.

Hi Mr. Alan,

Sorry I haven't e-mailed you in awhile. School has me really busy. I just took the GMAT last weekend and now I'm working on my application to an MBA Program.

If it's not too much trouble, I was hoping you would write a letter of recommendation for me. Additionally, I have attached the form you need to fill out and my resume.

If you need anything else or if you have any questions, please let me know.

Thank you in advance,

Yuri

No matter who the students are, no matter what the color of their skin, no matter how much money their parents have or do not have in the bank, educators must expect the world from them even when storm clouds make it appear as if the light of day is forever dimming.

Sure, it's been said a thousand times before but it most certainly deserves repeating yet again: we must set the highest of expectations for all children.

Tips for Teaching Teens to Seek Excellence

Exemplify

I hate to tell other teachers how they ought to conduct themselves, but the truth is there is simply no way to teach teens to seek excellence unless you yourself are striving to be an excellent educator at the front of the room.

Why? Because excellence resonates. It seeps. Like water, the intention to be excellent fills the cracks, gaps, and holes we inevitably run across as leaders of a classroom. And just as the smoker who preaches "You gotta take care of your health" has zero credibility to instruct others on their personal health habits, teachers who urge teens to "Try harder" when they do not exemplify outstanding work themselves—or at least an outstanding work ethic—will be undercut by their own hypocrisy.

Teens are pretty good at identifying a charlatan, yet they're also pretty responsive to those who reach out to help them. Today's teachers have to know that "Do what I say, not what I do" is the most hollow form of instruction there is.

Before educators can preach excellence, they must seek to embody it in an aspect of their professional life teens can clearly see as action and not just hear as words. An old storyteller's rule is "Show, don't tell." When it comes to excellence, this is something a teacher must always keep in mind.

Show How Seeking Excellence Is a Bridge to a Teen's Biggest Dreams

As a teacher I know that it's rarely natural skill sets that separate A students from C+ pupils but rather the effort they give toward being excellent. That is the great difference maker. What teens need to know is that people who persistently strive to be outstanding at what they do inevitably reach the top of whatever mountain they are working to climb

For the teens who doubt this, have them brainstorm a list of their three favorite role models. If there is one quality I've discovered all role models seem to have in common, it's a sense of excellence. They may be excellent performers, excellent businesspeople, excellent mechanics, or excellent thieves, but no one idolizes mediocrity. It's simply not worth celebrating.

There are no two ways about it. Teenagers who strive to be excellent shine like diamonds against black velvet. Competency takes us only so far. The pursuit of excellence, on the other hand, has wings on which we soar.

Teach Teens That People Who Seek Excellence Are Rare

The fact is people who actually strive to be outstanding are few and far between, and while corporate logos try to fill our heads with propaganda about how customer service is number one, there are times when we all take airline flights, call cell phone companies, or walk into retail chain stores and wonder if the CEOs of these corporations ever actually use any of the services their companies tout as being top o' the heap. Heck, I go out to eat. I wait in express lines at supermarkets. I deal with multinational conglomerates that route my phone calls to foreign countries where those who pick up try to tell me everything is fine when it most clearly isn't (after I spend 17 minutes in voice-mail hell).

It's maddening. But worse, it makes for very few examples that teens can use as paradigms for their own attitudes and behavior.

Teach teens not to be a part of the status quo; it gets you nowhere, it's unfulfilling, and, most abominably, it's a sad and boring way to go through the world. Seek to be excellent or move out of the way because soon enough, someone will be passing you by.

Watch for the Three Enemies of Seeking Excellence

Mistaking the Pursuit of Excellence for Mandating Perfection

No one is saying anybody has to be perfect. No one is saying that anyone has to be faultless. No one is saying that anyone must be error free. These are unrealistic demands that may inhibit success as opposed to enabling it because unattainable dictates cause teens to lose ambition rather than gain inspiration toward achieving their goals.

Teens need to understand that the real pursuit of excellence is often sloppy. It's messy. It's filled with errors, backtracking, hole patching, and sausage making. Eliminate the quest for impeccability by making it clear that perfection is unattainable, mistakes are tools from which we all learn, and excellence is best measured by the dedication and commitment shown along the journey of performance, not final results.

The pursuit of perfection is paralyzing. Give your students open-ended permission to make mistakes; it relieves pressures, allows people to experiment, and frees teens to actually push harder, probe deeper, and attain greater heights.

The Light Switch Mentality

Excellence is a habit, a by-product of perpetually striving toward ambitious aims. However, outstanding performance is not a light switch that gets turned on and off whenever teens suddenly feel inspired to give it their all; rather, it's the result of a steady stream of consummate, outstanding, give-it-all-you've-got efforts, efforts that are grounded in the intention to be excellent before one even embarks on the journey.

And like a muscle, this intention needs constant and vigorous toning in order to deliver results.

Watch out for teens who feel that they'll be able to step up to the big challenges while coasting through the smaller ones with a mediocre exertion of labor and energy. As all champion athletes know, trophies are won with intense sweat on the practice field before the big game even starts, far away from the lights and cameras of the big stage. There is no light switch when it comes to seeking excellence. Teens need to cultivate the mental habit of doing all things to the best of their ability because ultimately excellence translates to all aspects of life.

A Bar Too Low

Years of classroom experience have taught me that when it comes to students, my own beliefs about what they can accomplish, who they can be, or how they can perform almost always far exceed their own beliefs about themselves. This is why it's so crucial to set the bar high and keep it high because, as I well know, whenever we accept a student doing less than a stellar job or giving less than a stellar effort, what we're really doing is delivering a subtextual message that says it's okay to stink, even if it is just a wee little bit.

And it's not. Not at all.

Not if they bake their grandmother a cake, not if they rake up the leaves on a lawn, and most certainly not if they do work toward accomplishing a classroom assignment. Shoddiness, as many teachers well know, is the slickest of slippery slopes, and nowhere is the phrase "Give them an inch and they'll take a mile" more true than in a middle or high school class-room.

Ultimately, excellence in education is the antithesis of boring. Great teaching teems with energy, excitement, and passion. It's where students are motivated, teachers are vibrant, and learning is an interactive, collaborative, nonlinear process that empowers all learners to move intellectual leaps and bounds beyond the mere rote memorization of stats, data, rules, and facts. Teens will rise to the expectations we hold for them.

Our expectations are the harbingers of their futures.

Appendices

The Physical Classroom as a Living, Breathing Collage

I view my classroom as a living, breathing space. It's growing, changing, shifting, and morphing all the time, a collage of colors, ideas, posters, jokes, quotes, quips, student work, pictures, thoughts, and ideas. Everywhere a person goes, there is something to catch the eye.

By my front door I have a wall of Far Side cartoons, which at the start of the year is something most students simply pass by. But as the year goes on, logjams of traffic by the door are created because so many students are blocking the pathway, reading the works of a man I consider to be one of the funniest cartoonists who ever lived. Students who never heard of Gary Larson before the year started become devoted fans before the school year is out.

As a matter of fact, I have jokes everywhere across my room. Tucked in corners, by the pencil sharpener, by my desk. Here's one collection that sits next to the recycling bin:

Question: Why do gorillas have big nostrils?

Answer: Because they have big fingers.

Question: What's the difference between roast beef and pea soup?

Answer: Anyone can roast beef.

Question: What do you call a hunk of cheddar that does not belong to you?

Answer: Nacho cheese.

Jokes promote reading, humor, and warmth and really help create an inviting, disarming environment.

I also have pictures of some of my favorite writers and thinkers posted all around. I have a great shot of Einstein playfully sticking his tongue out, a poster of Abraham Lincoln with the quote "Most people are about as happy as they make up their minds to be," and a 5-foot-tall full-length poster of the grandmaster himself, William Shakespeare, watching over us all.

There's also a Wall of Acceptance Letters, filled with photocopies of students' college acceptance letters to universities across America, including the University of Southern California, Stanford, Berkeley, Amherst, UC San Diego, Pepperdine, Loyola Marymount, and MIT, among others, so my students can see the accomplishments of other students from Lynwood who once sat in the very same chairs they are now sitting in themselves.

One year I even brought in a donated couch and a few garage sale beanbags to make Readin' Time more comfortable for my teens. (And what a smash success it's been. I wish I'd thought of it years earlier.) Truly, who doesn't prefer a soft couch to a hard, plastic chair? (I only wish they'd let me shop for all my own classroom furniture.)

There are computers I've scavenged over the years from all sorts of people and places, posters for the opera, ad campaigns for hip-hop festivals, *National Geographic* pictures of wild animals, and a poster of Picasso's famous painting *Guernica* from the Museo del Prado, which I purchased the last time I was in Spain. I even have a poster on my ceiling from Michelangelo's Sistine Chapel for kids to check out when they look up.

Literally, it would take hours to read all the material I have on the walls of my classroom. And every year, I make sure to invite my new students to find a way to contribute to the mélange. They post student work, find funny cartoons of their own in magazines, or bring me university pins from the college tours I always encourage them to take.

In my estimation, a colorful, rich, full classroom sets the tone for a colorful, rich educational experience. And students, I've discovered, are much less likely to deface and tag up my room because the walls are so warm and welcoming. A physical environment that makes students feel accepted and respected is a tool, an additional ally I use to accomplish all of the many goals I have for my teens throughout the year.

Three Things Teens Can Do to Have a Great School Year

Do Their Homework

I'm not sure when it happened, but far too many students think that homework is an option. It's not. All truly successful students do their homework. Not some of their homework. Not most of their homework. *All* of their homework. I don't teach half of my students. Restaurants don't serve most of my dinner. The IRS doesn't require me to pay 65 percent of my taxes. In the real world, real jobs require that 100 percent of the assigned tasks be completed. Teenagers need to do all of their homework. If they do, I guarantee that these kids will see their efforts directly reflected in a very positive manner both on their report cards and in their academic growth. The connection from strong, consistent homework to strong, consistent grades is a straight line. Remember, homework is not an option.

Be Productive After School

The hours between 3:00 P.M. and 7:00 P.M. might be the most critical in a teenager's day. Study after study shows that this is the time slot when kids who merely hang out get into the most trouble. Trouble can mean anything from doing drugs to having sex to getting involved with gangs or running seriously afoul of the law. Less obvious but certainly very problematic pitfalls during these after-school witching hours also include kids simply melting their brains away by watching hour upon hour of mindless TV or playing video games or surfing the Internet until their cerebral cortexes have been reduced to mush. (Of course they do this while consuming enough junk food to start their very own 7-Eleven, too.) After-school participation in something that is meaningful and of genuine interest to a teenager—the arts, a club, a hobby, sports, *something*—is crucial to them having a successful school year. Don't worry so much about academics; there will be plenty of classwork over the course of a year. And plenty of tests, as well. However, making sure that young people are involved in something concrete, something extracurricular—photography, piano, gymnastics—that occupies this vital time slot in their day is the key to keeping kids on the right path while staying away from a host of potential problems. Remember, in today's world, just kickin' it can be a recipe for disaster.

Use a Planner

I can't tell you how crazy it drives me to see teenagers write down homework assignments on the backs of their hands or the sides of their folders or, worse yet, swear to me (as they squinch their eyes and try to cement my assignment in their brains) that they'll "remember" it. Students shouldn't need to remember it. Their craniums should be occupied with more important thinking activities than simply trying to remember class assignments. A planner allows for organization (and organization is, as many adults know, a prerequisite to success). A planner allows for simplicity (everything is always in the same place so there is never a need to wonder where that sticky note with math homework on it disappeared to). A planner allows parents to actually see what kids need to do and by when (thus eliminating the question "Do you have any homework tonight?" forevermore—parents can just look in their kids' planners). Planners empower students to be successful, and teens who use them inevitably find that their school year becomes both less stressful and more productive. A planner is the small tool that unquestionably paves the way for great student achievement.

Teenagers are going to have to take a degree of ownership over their own education. Parents and teachers cannot do it for them. However, parents and teachers can (and should) support them in a way that enables teens to enjoy a school year filled with both personal and academic success. Having teens do the three things listed here will most assuredly start their upcoming school year off on the right foot.

Back-to-School-Night Tips to Pass Along to Parents

I am always looking for ways I can help parents help their own kids to do well in school (and life), so I put together a small but helpful tip sheet that is nice to give out at events such as open house or back-to-school night.

🟤 Three Things Parents Can Do to Make Sure Their Kids Have a Great School Year

Make Sure Your Teens Have a Quiet Place and a Regular Time to Study

Teachers give homework. Parents expect homework. Students need to do homework. However, without a designated place and time where students can actually do their homework, the system breaks down. Ask yourself the following questions: "Does my child have a location where he or she can work in peace and quiet? Does my child have a regular time slot when she or he can be expected to do the work that has been assigned?" A consistent homework location and a consistent homework time in a consistently homework-friendly environment (i.e., no phone, no MySpace, no television) is something your kids might not necessarily recognize that they need, nor know how to create for themselves. Yet as a parent, it is your job to create a space, place, and schedule so that your teen can be successful.

Take a Good Look at Your Teenager's Friends

The truth is friends are incredibly important to teenagers, and the amount of influence peers have on the decisions that your child will eventually make is much larger than most parents ever want

---

to believe. Know your teen's friends! Know who they are. Know what they are doing. Know their habits of character, personality, and school. (It's not that hard to find out. Usually, a few minutes of conversation with any young person will clue you in on all you need to know.) Now, will teens try to pull the wool over the eyes of adults? Of course. This is why if red flags go up, you should trust your instincts and take action. While your teenager may not be immediately receptive to the fact that you are doing this, this is what good parenting is: getting involved and warding off trouble *before* it happens. Like attracts like, and teens who hang around with good kids usually turn out to be good kids as well.

Set High Expectations for Your Child, the Teachers, and the School

If 200 students complain about something on campus, nothing happens. If 20 teachers complain about something on campus, things might happen. If 2 parents complain about something on campus, mountains move. This is because when you are a parent, you are the boss. Everyone in education works for you, and if you let us slide (*us* being the kids, the teachers, or the school), we probably will. However, if you set the bar high and insist that we rise to the occasion, you will discover that we may not bat a thousand, but we certainly will put in that extra zing to work toward meeting your expectations. Parents who set high standards and make them clearly known right at the start of the year often see that people rise to meet their expectations. And parents who don't do this at the start of the year often turn into complainers who wish things were different. I am not saying you get to run the school, but I am saying that you most certainly have a powerful voice in how the school runs. Set high expectations. Hey, when it comes to my own kids, I most certainly do.

Years of experience at the front of the classroom have shown me that students who do the three things I strongly suggest, combined with parents who do the three things I strongly suggest, almost always have productive, meaningful years.

Getting Teens to Recognize the Wheres and Whens of Appropriate Language

Not all language is appropriate for all circumstances. I certainly don't speak to my college buddies, for example, in the same tone (or with the same word choices) I would use to speak to the president of the company that published this book. This is because people are multidialectical; that is, they speak to different audiences with different vernaculars and different levels of formality, depending on the occasion.

Unfortunately, though, my students often use the same language, tone, and word choices for their essay assignments as they use in their lunchtime make-fun-of-someone's-momma goof-around sessions.

And it's not appropriate.

Therefore, I have to teach the skill of differentiating the where and when of proper usage. In class, particularly when writing, we use the queen's English. Outside of class, well . . . I don't want to know. (Truthfully, some of the language teens use these days in the halls would burn your ears off.) I teach my students how to differentiate the wheres and whens of language usage through the fine art of complaining.

"Have you ever bought something that was just a hunk of junk?" I ask my class.

Kids nod, hands go up, and kids start to yap about all sorts of things.

"Wait, wait," I say, "let's do this: everybody partner up into groups of two or three and let's all compose a text message complaining to the person who sold you this piece of garbage."

Of course in a Title I school, not all of my students have cell phones—heck, not all of them eat breakfast—but breaking them off into small groups allows them to share phones if they need to.

Once my students have a bit of fun creating a "txt mssg 2 a *PUNK!*" I have them each take out a sheet of paper and transcribe their text message, word for word, letter for letter, and character for character.

Then I split the class down the middle and on a different piece of paper have each student write the same letter of complaint about the product to a partner across the room, as if the partner were the party responsible for producing or selling this hunk of junk. However, for this stage of the project, the complaint is to be written in the style of passing a class note, the kind that teachers aren't supposed to see.

Goodness, do they love this! And since I tell them that I am not going to collect these notes and they can really write them in the clandestine style in which they'd typically author such a thing (*clandestine* is a great vocabulary word that almost always shows up on the SAT), my kids set eagerly to work.

Then they trade the notes and lots of laughs ensue.

I, of course, do not look at the notes. "Don't ask, don't tell," is the policy that guides this stage of class. Plus, it builds trust. I tell them I will not read their notes, and I don't. Small things like this go a long way over the course of a school year.

Next, I have my students compose an e-mail. However, since I don't yet have enough computers for all my students to do this, sometimes I make it a homework assignment and sometimes I just have them handwrite the e-mail in order to keep things moving along. When you're a teacher, you play a lot of things by ear.

After the e-mails are composed, I put a graphic organizer on the board and we compare and contrast the similarities and differences between a text message, a classroom note, and an e-mail.

By the way, participation through this point of the assignment is almost always 100 percent, a level I frequently struggled to achieve when it came to writing before I converted to the academic camp of "always meet them first where they are."

Once we've covered the idea that there are different writing styles that go along with different modes of writing (i.e., the text message, the e-mail, and the class note, while similar, use different modes of expression), I tell my class that we are now going to write a real letter of complaint to the real company that originally sold them the unsatisfactory item. It may have been a terrible cheeseburger they picked up in the local drive-through but didn't return because it would have taken too much effort to deal with once they were already home. It may have been a shirt they bought that tore at the seams after the first wash. It may have been a toy that broke after their baby sister played with it for only five minutes. It matters little what their letter of complaint is about. What matters is that my students understand that there is a standard of appropriateness for each different style of writing, one that differs between text messaging, passing classroom notes, and e-mailing.

As I point out once we have moved on to the business letter stage (by the way, I've just elevated this activity to a standards-based writing project), some forms of writing have slang, sloppiness, profanity, and almost a contemporary sense of hieroglyphs, while other forms of writing require a formality, decorum, and measured level of appropriateness.

Unfortunately, my students' knowledge and experience of when and where to apply these different forms are all jumbled up before we do this activity. Afterward, my kids can discern the differences.

Sadly, more and more teens these days do not differentiate between requisite writing styles, and as a result, their academic ability to succeed in a world that unequivocally values the use of proper language convention is hampered. So when I ask my kids to begin with text messages, what I'm really doing is tapping their prior knowledge about writing in order to build a bridge to the knowledge they need to acquire formal writing.

And all of this is accomplished while having fun, keeping the students engaged, and following the prescribed content area mandates of my state.

Ultimately, we mail the letters, and when the students get responses back in the mail, they never fail to bring them in to share with everybody. The joy of acknowledgment from companies like Entenmann's bakery, Mead Paper Company, and the Gap does wonders for my students' self-esteem and further highlights how the pen can be a mighty tool when wielded properly.

The Spice in the Secret Sauce

I am always seeking to connect my teens' out-of-class interests to the in-class academic work we will be studying. One of my most successful tools for accomplishing this comes from asking myself, "What's the spicy, get-my-kids-going question that will light this class on fire?" Here are a few effective questions:

- Should our school pass out condoms to students?

- If you found $500,000 in cash in a briefcase in the bushes on your way home from school, what would you do? (By the way, the handle of the briefcase is covered in blood.)

- If your best friend was in a deep coma and you were the person chosen to make the decision about whether to pull the plug, would you? Or would you allow your best friend to live in a vegetative state for years and years to come?

Now, these are not just salacious questions. In my opinion, questions like these are doorways to get my students to talk, think, write, or debate. And questions such as these work exceptionally well because they revolve around subjects my students care about. Or have an interest in. Or find exciting, dangerous, taboo, or just flat-out intriguing.

The first question, about passing out condoms, is something I ripped straight from the news. It's a very real debate raging in communities across the country. I figure, "Why not have my own students participate?"

The second question, about the briefcase full of money, comes from a creative writing prompt I designed to invite my students to weave a tale of mystery, imagination, and suspense as we worked on adding more salient details to our writing and storytelling.

The third question is an offshoot from the book *Stuck in Neutral* (Trueman 2000), which we read in class, a story about a boy in a wheelchair who thinks his father is planning to kill him out of a misguided sense of euthanasia.

All of these spicy questions always lead to very interesting discussions, which makes English class feel relevant, exciting, and not boring.

As I've seen time and time again, when teenagers are faced with questions like these, they want to express their opinions. And they want to hear the opinions of other teens, too. Spicy questions, I've realized, get my class going. They turn reluctant participants into active listeners and contributors.

> ● **Should America welcome the children of illegal immigrants into our public schools free of charge?**
>
> ● **Should marijuana be legalized?**
>
> ● **Are violent video games causing violence in society?**

Questions like these are exceptionally flexible, too. I can divide the room by gender and stage a debate, I can sit all kids at their desks and have them complete detailed graphic organizers to make them think deeply and widely about an issue, or I can section my class off into pieces of a jigsaw and have them each look at one of the spicy issues from a multitude of perspectives (e.g., the legalization of marijuana from the perspective of a police officer, a person suffering from glaucoma, the religious mom of a rebellious teen, and an IRS agent who sees the potential tax revenue that could be generated by legalizing and taxing all sales of pot).

When teens are asked spicy questions, their urge to respond is virtually irrepressible. How they respond, though—the format, the mode, and the means—is entirely up to the teacher. Papers, projects, debates, conversations, they're all at my fingertips (as are the content standards). But the key is building up a response energy inside teenagers that they feel compelled to release.

Get teens working through spicy questions, and your challenge won't be how to engage your students in class but rather how to manage their electric enthusiasm!

Getting Teens to Discover Their Own Strengths: The Seven Intelligences

A ll teenagers have unique strengths and aptitudes, and while it's important for me to learn where each student feels most competent, it's much more important that my teens learn for themselves where they perform best, so they can eventually steer their lives in that direction. This is why I always introduce my students to the ideas of Howard Gardner and allow them to identify for themselves their own strengths, aptitudes, learning styles, and distinct intelligences.

Although people learn in different ways, our schools in general have been slow to recognize and respond appropriately to these differences. As Gardner himself has noted, kids who have greater mathematical-logical and linguistic intelligences are frequently rewarded by our school systems, while students whose strengths lie elsewhere often go unrecognized and unrewarded. (Not coincidentally, the mathematical-logical skills are also the most testable strengths.)

I use Gardner's theory of multiple intelligences to validate my students' abilities so they can reflect on who they are and work toward developing their strengths—and avoid banging their heads against the wall, trying to becoming something they are not. Ultimately, when we feel valued and competent, we perform accordingly.

Unfortunately, I'm not able to differentiate my whole curriculum to serve the learning styles of all students on every assignment I make, but over the course of the school year, I try to make sure that I tap all seven intelligences so that every learning style has a chance to be acknowledged, recognized, and validated in my classroom.

The Seven Intelligences: Which One Best Suits Your Students?

Harvard psychologist Howard Gardner has identified seven distinct types of intelligence, or learning styles (Condor n.d.).

Linguistic Intelligence

Linguistic intelligence deals with words. This is the primary intelligence for storytellers, journalists, and attorneys. It provides the foundation to effectively inform, persuade, argue, teach, and entertain. Kids high in this intelligence will be proficient with word games and tongue twisters. They will enjoy the sounds of words and tend to be avid readers and clear writers.

Logical-Mathematical Intelligence

Not surprisingly, this is the mind's ability to work with numbers and logical sequencing. Think scientists, accountants, software developers. Kids with this intelligence set will be good at understanding cause and effect, numerical patterns, and rationales (which could come in handy in dealing with the parents, too).

Spatial Intelligence

This covers the ability to conceptualize in mental images and pictures. Typical careers are in photography and art. These kids are good at visual details and tend to draw graphics and 3-D images that seem beyond their years. A key facet is the child's ability to transfer those mental pictures to a form the rest of us can see.

Musical Intelligence

Pretty straightforward, this is the gift of grasping and producing rhythms and melodies. One way to identify musical intelligence is determining if a child can discern between two relatively similar pieces of music. Musician represents one obvious career path, but we all know adults who have good ears and can sing in tune. So it may be that this intelligence is part of life-long learning rather than a career track.

Bodily-Kinesthetic Intelligence

This intelligence type is hard for some traditionalists to accept. But agility and dexterity clearly originate from somewhere, and Gardner connects these attributes to the mind. Kids who are hands-on learners possess it and could well become athletes, mechanics, surgeons, or carpenters. They are good knitters if given the chance and love to build models. These kids tend to be self-starters in gym class and during physical activities. An interesting note from Gardner's work: people with high bodily-kinesthetic intelligence are most likely to have instinctual gut reactions.

Intrapersonal Intelligence

This is the domain of the inner self. Kids in this category are able to identify their feelings and distinguish various shades of the same emotion. It is an intelligence we all come to appreciate as we become adults—the idea of understanding and accepting ourselves. Intrapersonal intelligence prompts soul searching, self-discipline, strong independence, and a tendency to set goals, but not necessarily all at one time or in one kid.

Interpersonal Intelligence

This brand of smarts is about working with others. These kids not only get along with classmates but show a capacity to recognize moods and needs of other people, including adults. They could well be better at it than their own parents. One caution: this is a good-evil proposition. The interpersonally intelligent child could be compassionate and get good-citizen marks on report cards or use the same intelligence to manipulate and outsmart others.

At www.mitest.com/o7inte~1.htm you'll find a seven intelligences checklist for youth ages 13–18, which can be scored online or printed out and scored by hand using a rubric. The checklist was developed by Spencer Barnard and modified by Nancy Faris.

No-Fail Books for Teens

I call this section "No Fail Books for Teens" but that's not really true. Not every one is going to like everything. This list is more of a resource of titles that have really grabbed my reluctant reading students in a very absorbing, very thorough, very didn't-think-I-could-ever-get-that-kid-to-read way. There are no guarantees but when it comes to fickle, *I hate to read* kids, these are my GO TO titles. And they almost always work.

The Absolutely True Diary of a Part-Time Indian by Sherman Alexie

The Alchemist by Paulo Coelho

Always Running: La Vida Loca: Gang Days in L. A. by Luis J. Rodriguez

Bringing Down the House: The Inside Story of Six M.I.T. Students Who Took Vegas for Millions by Ben Mezrich

Bronx Masquerade by Nikki Grimes

A Child Called "It": One Child's Courage to Survive by Dave Pelzer

Crank by Ellen Hopkins

Cut by Patricia McCormick

Diary of a Wimpy Kid by Jeff Kinney

Ender's Game by Orson Scott Card

The Far Side Gallery (any book in the series) by Gary Larson

Fences by August Wilson

The First Part Last by Angela Johnson

Freak the Mighty by Rodman Philbrick

The Giver by Lois Lowry

Go Ask Alice by Anonymous

The Gun by Paul Langan

Hip-Hop High School by Alan Sitomer

Holes by Louis Sachar

Homeboyz by Alan Sitomer

The Hoopster by Alan Sitomer

Illusions: The Adventures of a Reluctant Messiah by Richard Bach

The Lion, the Witch, and the Wardrobe by C.S. Lewis

Monster by Walter Dean Myers

Oh Yuck! The Encyclopedia of Everything Nasty by Joy Masoff

The Outsiders by S. E. Hinton

The Pigman by Paul Zindel

The Power of One: A Novel by Bryce Courtenay

The Rose That Grew From Concrete by Tupac Shakur

The Secret Story of Sonia Rodriguez by Alan Sitomer

The Seven Habits of Highly Effective Teens by Sean Covey

The Skin I'm In by Sharon G. Flake

Speak by Laurie Halse Anderson

Stuck in Neutral by Terry Trueman

Tears of a Tiger by Sharon M. Draper

True Believer: A Novel in the Make Lemonade Trilogy by Virginia Euwer Wolff

The True Confessions of Charlotte Doyle by Avi

True Notebooks: A Writer's Year at Juvenile Hall by Mark Salzman

Tweak by Nic Sheff

Twilight: The Twilight Saga, Book 1 by Stephenie Meyer

On Writing

People often ask me how I improve the writing skills of the students in my classroom. The fact is it begins and ends with getting my teenagers to give an authentic effort toward their work. That's the first rule. Get kids to try. Really try. It's how I move a student's writing from this:

> The people I hung out this
> vacation with are with my three
> cusins from texas, One of them
> is a cool person, she's a nice person
> to hang out with, and she has a good
> haert, My other cusin I hung out with

To this, by the same student a few months later:

> What did I do over Spring Break?
> One of the things I did over Spring Break
> is I worked every day in the house,
> fixing, cleaning, and painting it. The second
> thing that I did over Spring Break was
> that I went out to parties and a wedding,
> The third thing that I did over Spring Break
> is that I spent some quality time with
> my uncle almost every day of my
> vacation.

And I achieve these results with kids all the time in the space of about half an academic year.

How? Because I start with hammering home the things that are first and foremost not beyond the scope of their abilities.

In my class we begin with making sure all of the words we use are spelled correctly. Dictionaries are available everywhere in my room; all a kid needs to do is reach under the desk, crack open a dictionary, and start flipping through the pages.

Then, we make sure all paragraphs we write are indented. Now, even though my kids may have heard all of this before, I still explain in meticulous detail to my entire class how to properly use the tab function on a computer keyboard as well as determine the proper length an indentation should have on a lined sheet of notebook paper.

It's a small lesson, one that takes but a few minutes. However, if I want my students to know it, then I'd better make sure I teach it to them. When you spend as much time remediating skills as I do, assumptions about prior knowledge are lesson killers. The fact is I just never know what my students know, what they don't know, and what they claim to know but really don't know. This is why I make sure to teach it all.

The capitalization of all letters that require being capitalized comes next. First letters of sentences, proper nouns versus common nouns, and, most critically, a complete and thorough explanation that students are never to use a lowercase i when the context requires an uppercase I to indicate the first person. Goodness, do I hammer this one home because nothing smacks of intellectual and academic laziness more to an English teacher than a kid writing, "When i go to the store. . . . " (However, the lowercase i compounded with misspellings like *wehn* for *when* is often my earliest indication that I am working with English language learners and need to differentiate my writing instruction so that it meets their individual needs as I keep the rest of the class going forward at a more advanced pace.)

Then I remind my students of such basics as using a period at the end of all their sentences. Or a question mark. Or an explanation point, should the occasion call for such a thing.

I also ban words such as *good*, *bad*, *really*, and *very* so that writers push a little deeper to utilize a more vivid and rich vocabulary.

And, yes, I do all of this at the high school level despite the fact that almost all of the skills I just cited are things my kids most probably first learned in either third or fourth grade.

But like many, many teachers of teenagers today, I don't see my kids applying these skills even though they have already learned them. And why?

The answer is not brains; it's effort.

That's my key to improving the literacy performance of kids who write with skills that test out at years below grade level. I get kids to buy in to the fact that they need to try. Really try.

When I ask my kids to put on big, bold display skills for me that (for the most part) they already have, I build their confidence and repair their oft-damaged writer's self-esteem. Then I can focus on the positive in their work and shower them with praise in an area of their lives where many of them have known only shame and belittlement. Beginning in this manner shows my kids that they are not bottom-dwelling academic dummies doomed to forever be illiterate and inarticulate but rather students who already possess appreciable skills that are developing, growing, and, with a little bit of elbow grease, going to be lifelong tools they'll possess, which no one will ever be able to take away from them.

For some of my teens, I am the first person in their lives who ever delivers this message to them. Quite naturally, it builds their pride, and once I tap this pride, and build the trust in my students that I am not simply going to red pen them to death by pointing out all their you-should-have-learned-that-years-ago mistakes, I become the beneficiary of positive momentum in my classroom. Once I even heard a wannabe boast, "Well, at least I ain't illiterate."

Of course, subject-verb agreement, the proper punctuation of appositive phrases, the logical organization of ideas within a paragraph, all these skills and many more come thereafter. But first, before my students can matriculate to this realm of academic accomplishment, they must give me a genuine effort toward being strong writers because without their own determination to succeed, I really have little chance of raising their performance levels.

No, it's not the quantity of writing that my students do that helps them raise their skills by such leaps and bounds in my class; it's the care and attention they give to details, to giving real effort, to taking responsibility for their own work and not loafing it through writing assignments just so they can get some credit for their work.

As famed business author Jim Collins (2001) once noted, "Good is the enemy of great." It's good—no, *great*—advice for the teaching of writing as well.

Not allowing students to accept mediocrity from themselves as writers is a key ingredient to raising their skills dramatically.

Six Tips for Teens to Avoid a Life of Poverty

1. Get an Education

A high school diploma is no longer enough. Teens today need to know that at least two years of learning beyond high school are virtually mandatory. It doesn't have to be college; it can be vocational training, an apprenticeship, or even self-study. However, the first two years of any new career need to be viewed as a period of learning.

Remember, you must spend time planting seeds before you can expect to harvest fruit (which is also why the more time teens spend pursuing their education after high school, the more likely it is that their eventual career earnings will increase dramatically).

2. Wait to Have Children Until You Are Old Enough to Drink Alcohol Legally

This is not moralizing. This has nothing to do with religion. The simple fact is that babies are extremely expensive and they can be a financial weight that forever prevents people from escaping the perils of poverty because of the nonstop financial obligations all kids inevitably bring with them.

Look, I love kids, but waiting to have them until there is a foundation in place to be able to afford them (and thus, better enjoy them, serve them, and raise them) is extremely prudent.

3. Don't Break the Law

America loves to send people to jail. As a matter of fact, we have done so more than any other society in the history of civilization. But going to prison is like putting a grape juice stain that never comes out on the T-shirt of life. It might fade, it can be covered up, but once it's there, it taints a person's existence—in a decidedly negative manner—for practically forever.

Employers in every industry frown on people with criminal records, and time spent in prison often limits future possibilities.

4. Choose Friends Who Are on the Road to Somewhere Positive

Friends are like moons with an irresistible gravitational pull. Good friends will pull a teen in positive directions; bad friends will pull a teen into low, undesirable places. Teens draw so much strength from their friends that choosing wisely becomes incredibly important. And as most adults know, true friends are often few and far between . . . so they must choose wisely.

5. Feed Yourself Mentally in a Consistent, Positive Manner

Put something positive, uplifting, informative, fun, or inspirational into your brain every day. Nothing better explains why it is so critical than this old Cherokee tale:

> *The Two Wolves*
> *One evening an old Cherokee was telling his grandson about the battle that goes on inside of all human beings.*
>
> *"It's a battle between two wolves," said the old man. "And they live within us all. One is evil," the old Cherokee warned. "It is made of anger, envy, jealousy, sorrow, regret, greed, arrogance, self-pity, guilt, resentment, lies, false pride, and ego."*

The young boy looked up with wide, fearful eyes.

"The other is good," continued the old man with a warm smile. "It is made up of joy, peace, love, hope, humility, kindness, generosity, truth, compassion, and faith."

The young boy sat silently for a minute, considering the story. A moment later, he raised his eyes. "But Grandfather, which wolf wins?" asked the child.

The old Cherokee replied, "The one you feed, my son. The one you feed."

6. Be Willing to Work Hard

The easy path often leads to hard-to-swallow destinations. I tell students, "Roll up your shirtsleeves, do what needs to be done, give a complete and total effort, and be willing to work your way to the top from the ground up." It's a simple formula that reaps direct, simple consequences because everyone loves a hard worker.

And hard workers, no matter how high the odds are stacked against them, always find a way to make their own breaks in life.

My "Come See Me" Policy

When students of mine, past and present, have problems, they know they can come see me.

When students of mine, past and present, need to print a paper for another class, they know they can come see me. After all, it's not really my computer they are asking to use anyway—it's theirs.

When students of mine, past and present, have trouble at home, they know they can come see me. After all, sometimes we just need to talk.

When students of mine, past and present, get kicked out of other classes, they know they can come see me. After all, it's better for me to remain open as a home for wayward kids than it is for wayward kids to feel as if they have no home.

When students of mine, past and present, need a letter of reference, they know they can come see me. After all, once upon a time when I was in high school, I needed letters of reference, too (though I'm not sure how many people really read them).

When students of mine, past and present, need anything, from endorsements for student council, to help deciphering which summertime internship program is best for them to pursue, to what to do when they can't keep up with their classes because their parents work multiple jobs and it's their responsibility to watch their younger siblings after school, they know they can come see me. I may not have all the answers, but I always try to help.

I have a "come see me" policy. While there are times the workload gets stacked extra high as a result of it, most times I find that for teenagers, it's simply enough to know that there is someone available for them to go see if they feel the need.

And sometimes, students come see me just to say hi. Having no reason to see me is sometimes the best reason of all.

References

Block, A., & Weisz, V. (2004, July 6). Choosing prisoners over pupils. *The Washington Post*, p. A19. Available: www.washingtonpost.com/ac2/wp-dyn/A29806-2004Jul5?language=printer.

Bradshaw, J. (2006). *Teenage births.* York, UK: Joseph Rowntree Foundation.

Bridgeland, J. M., DiIulio, J. J., & Morison, K. B. (2006, March). *The silent epidemic: Perspectives of high school dropouts.* Seattle, WA: Bill and Melinda Gates Foundation. Available: www.gatesfoundation.org/nr/downloads/ed/thesilentepidemic3 06final.pdf.

Burke, Jim. (2008). *The teacher's essential guide: Classroom instruction.* New York: Scholastic.

Child Trends Databank. (2005, October). *Dropout rates and number and percentage distribution of dropouts ages 16 to 24, selected characteristics.* Washington, DC: Child Trends Databank. Available: www.childtrendsdatabank.org/indicators/1highschooldropout.cfm.

Coley, R. L., & Chase-Lansdale, P. L. (1998). Adolescent pregnancy and parenthood: Recent evidence and future directions. *American Psychologist, 53*(2), 152–166.

Collins, J. (2001). *Good to great: Why some companies make the leap . . . and others don't.* New York: HarperBusiness.

Condor, B. (n.d.). Lucky seven. MSN Health & Fitness. Available: http://health.msn.com/kids-health/articlpage.aspx?cp-documentid=1001558738page=1

Courtenay, Bryce. (1989). *The power of one: A novel.* New York: Ballantine.

Covey, Sean. (1998). *The 7 habits of highly effective teens.* New York: Fireside.

Covey, Stephen R. (2004). *The 7 habits of highly effective people: Powerful lessons in personal change.* New York: Free Press.

Day, J. C., & Newburger, E. C. (2002). The big payoff: Educational attainment and synthetic estimates of work-life earnings. (Current Population Reports, Special Studies, P23-210). Washington, DC: Commerce Dept., Economics and Statistics Administration, Census Bureau. Available: www.census.gov/prod/2002pubs/p23-210.pdf.

Eckholm, E. (2006, March 20). Plight deepens for black men, studies warn: Growing disconnection from the mainstream. Available: www.nytimes.com/2006/03/20/national/20blackmen.html.

Eshbaugh, E. (2008). Maternal age and depressive symptoms in a low income sample. *Journal of Community Psychology, 36*(3), 399–409.

Hendricks, C. G., Hendricks, J. E., & Kauffman, S. (2001). Literacy, criminal activity, and recidivism. *American reading forum online yearbook* (Vol. xxi). Boone, NC: American Reading Forum. Available: http://americanreadingforum.org/01_ yearbook/html/12_Hendricks.htm.

Landsberg, M. (2006, January). The vanishing class. *Los Angeles Times.*

Martin, N., & Halperin, S. (2006). Every nine seconds in America a student becomes a dropout. *Whatever it takes: How twelve communities are reconnecting out-of-school youth* (pp. vii–ix). Washington, DC: American Youth Policy Forum.

Myers-Lipton, S. (2006). *Social solutions to poverty: America's struggle to build a just society.* Boulder, CO: Paradigm Publishers. Available: www.solvingpoverty.com/ PovertyFacts.htm.

National Institute for Literacy. (1998). *The state of literacy in America: Estimates at the local, state, and national levels.* FL: Municipalities.

Ohanian, S. (1982, August). There's only one true technique for good discipline. *Learning, 11*(1), 16–19.

Passel, J., & Cohn, D. (2008, February 11). *Immigration to play lead role in future U.S. growth: U.S. population projections: 2000–2050.* Washington, DC: Pew Research Center. Available: http://pewresearch.org/pubs/729/united-states-population-projections.

Richard, A. (2005, November 2). Researchers tally costs of education failing. New York: Campaign for Education Equity at Teachers College, Columbia University. Available: www.tc.columbia.edu/news/article.htm?id=5343.

Ross, J. (2007, October). How does California compare? Funding California's public schools. *School finance facts.* Sacramento, CA: California Budget Project. Available: www.cbp.org/pdfs/2007/071009_howdoescacompare.pdf.

Snow, C. E., & Ninio, A. (1986). The contracts of literacy: What children learn from learning to read books. In W. H. Teale & E. Sulzby (Eds.), *Emergent literacy: Writing and reading* (pp. 116–137). Norwood, NJ: Ablex.

Snyder, T. D., Dillow, S. A., & Hoffman, C. M. (2007). Table 88: Revenues, expenditures, poverty rate, and Title I allocations of public school districts enrolling more than 15,000 students, by state: 2003–04 and fiscal year 2006. *Digest of education statistics: 2006.* Washington, DC: National Center for Education Statistics. Available: http://nces.ed.gov/programs/digest/d06/tables/dt06_088.asp.

Swanson, C. B. (2004, February 25). Who graduates? Who doesn't? A statistical portrait of public high school graduation, class of 2001. Available: www.urban. org/url.cfm?ID=410934.

Trueman, T. (2000). *Stuck in neutral.* New York: HarperCollins Children's Books.

Wells, C. G. (1985). Preschool literacy-related activities and success in school. In D. Olson, N. Torrance, & A. Hildyard (Eds.), *Literacy, language, and learning: The nature and consequences of literacy* (pp. 229–255). Cambridge, UK: Cambridge University Press.

Letter to Lynwood

A special note to all my friends and students in Lynwood.

Those who know me know that I absolutely LOVE working at Lynwood High School. I've been there a long time, developed special relationships with more people than I could ever dream to list, and discovered more beauty in this world than I ever knew existed as a result of my time spent as a teacher in Room 6213. And though I have been offered jobs at other schools, I always turn them down because the grass for me is not greener.

I love Lynwood High.

However, our school has its share of challenges; challenges that are in no way unique to Lynwood High but rather emblematic of issues public middle and high schools face all across the country. From Chicago to Baltimore to Philadelphia to Miami to Oakland to Brooklyn to Detroit, schools are confronted with the same hurdles that loom before us. That's why I wrote this book.

I have an inkling I can help.

Please know that I have no aim to insult, hurt, offend, or cause injury in any shape or form whatsoever to any of the people, professionals, or persons in the community where I teach. Yet, as the California Department of Education has proven through an analysis of our data, our school—like so many others across the state and nation—is experiencing certain painful truths that are caught in the spotlight I shine in this book. I shine the light first, to share the beauty of our institution. I've held a lot of jobs prior to being a teacher and nowhere have I seen so many people working so hard to do so much with so little. On the whole, we deserve praise, not scorn, and I wanted to author a book that made this point loud and clear to anyone who would listen to me. We do have our areas of difficulty, though, and they can be tough to examine with an open heart and mind.

I believe that the only way to remediate, rectify, and really address what is literally a crisis in far too many of America's schools—not just in the 90262 zip code—is to lay matters out so that others can see the issues and that together, in earnest, we can work for solutions. And I talk so freely about Lynwood in this book because I believe Lynwood is a place that wants to be better, wants to improve, and wants people to know about how much genuine good is going on inside its halls and classrooms. Sure, some of the realities are tough, but people from Lynwood are tough, too, and I have all the confidence in the world that the good heart, good character, and good intentions of the people who live, work, and attend school in our community will take pride in Lynwood High when the final page of this book has been turned and read.

Furthermore, know that I have changed the names and kept private all the identities of all our students so that there are no negative repercussions for any real people about whom I discuss. These are my students, and I love them.

My students have made me a better human being and it is my strongest belief that all readers of this book will also fall in love with the heart, beauty, tenacity, and all-around goodness of Lynwood's students by the time all is said and done.

As I mention in the text, at the end of the day, we all work for the students. To borrow a quote we hear all the time around my district, "Kids can't wait."

Well, it's true. Our kids—and by that I mean our nation's kids—deserve more, they deserve better, and I hope with all my heart that my efforts will in some measure contribute to the positive changes our country's schools so desperately need.

With much affection,
Mr. Alan